TECHNICAL ASSISTANCE

BY RELIGIOUS AGENCIES IN LATIN AMERICA

TECHNICAL ASSISTANCE

BY RELIGIOUS AGENCIES IN LATIN AMERICA

By James G. Maddox

 THE UNIVERSITY OF CHICAGO PRESS

Library of Congress Catalog Number: 56-6643

THE UNIVERSITY OF CHICAGO PRESS, CHICAGO 37
Cambridge University Press, London, N.W. 1, England
The University of Toronto Press, Toronto 5, Canada

© *1956 by The University of Chicago. Published 1956
Composed and printed by* THE UNIVERSITY OF CHICAGO
PRESS, *Chicago, Illinois, U.S.A.*

FOREWORD

By 1953, a number of public agencies and private groups in the United States were sharing their knowledge and skills with the people and governments of other countries. Most of them, however, were working independently. While it seemed likely that technical co-operation programs could become an increasingly constructive element in international co-operation, all too little was known about them. No thorough organized effort had been made to determine the extent to which this sharing of useful knowledge was helping the underdeveloped countries to help themselves or to see what its benefits—tangible and intangible—were to the United States.

Discussion with informed leaders in this field and with policy-makers, administrators, and technicians who were actively at work in public and private technical co-operation programs clearly indicated that a review and evaluation of the purposes, methods, and results of such programs would have wide usefulness, in both administering present programs and planning new ones. It was felt, further, that all concerned would have greater confidence in the findings if a critical analysis were made by an independent organization not involved with any of the public and private programs.

The National Planning Association's decision to undertake a far-reaching study of technical co-operation programs in order to gauge their potentialities and limitations in Latin America grew out of these discussions. The study was purposely concentrated on activities in Latin America—not because they were necessarily the most important or the best programs in the world, but because technical co-operation programs have been under way longer there than elsewhere and, until recent years, on a larger scale. Also, a great diversity of programs has been developed in Latin America. This diversity came about because the programs were created under a wide variety of auspices and conditions—sponsored by private foundations, the government of the United States, international organiza-

v

537907

tions, religious groups, universities, and business firms—each with somewhat different objectives. The programs also differ because the level and pace of development vary greatly from one Latin-American country to another, as do the political and social settings in which the programs operate. It was hoped that an intensive study of the rich experiences of the public agencies and private groups which have sponsored these programs under such diverse and complex circumstances would furnish important practical guides for technical co-operation.

The main objectives established for the NPA Project on Technical Co-operation in Latin America were:

1. To find out whether technical co-operation programs are making and can make a significant contribution to the long-range interests of the United States and of Latin-American countries in international understanding and growing international prosperity.

2. To identify the present objectives of public and private programs and judge their merits; to weigh results achieved in terms of such objectives; and to indicate standards for deciding which programs have greatest future value for the people of Latin America and of the United States.

3. To clarify the role of public technical co-operation programs in relation to private programs.

4. To point out ways and means of increasing the effectiveness of technical co-operation programs, of improving their administration, and of attracting and training competent and dedicated personnel for the programs.

Early in 1953, the Ford Foundation made a grant of $440,000 to finance the NPA Project on Technical Co-operation in Latin America. The Ford Foundation is not, however, to be understood as approving by virtue of its grant any of the views expressed in the research studies or the policy statements growing out of the project.

In accordance with NPA's established procedures, a Special Policy Committee on Technical Co-operation was formed to help plan the project, to consider the products of staff research, and to make recommendations on policy issues that confront the United States and Latin America in the fields of technical co-operation. This committee is composed of United States and Latin-American leaders from agriculture, business, labor, education, health, and other fields, to insure that its recommendations take into account the experience and views of such broadly based representative groups. Laird Bell, a senior partner of Bell, Boyd, Marshall and Lloyd in Chicago and a trustee of NPA, is chairman of the Special Policy Committee.

Theodore W. Schultz, of the University of Chicago and also a trustee of NPA, has organized the plan of study as director of research and has selected the research staff and consultants of the project. He and the research associates have done field work in twenty Latin-American republics, where they have made surveys and examined the records. They have consulted with business firms, religious bodies, foundations, universities, and other private organizations, as well as with government officials both of Latin-American countries and of the United States and with representatives of the Organization of American States, the United Nations, and its specialized agencies. A number of staff reports, incorporating the findings of the research effort, are being prepared. These reports are to be published at irregular intervals by the University of Chicago Press. Subjects of monographs and the authors are: Philip M. Glick on the administration of technical co-operation; Armando Samper on technical co-operation activities in the field of education; George I. Blacksten on the relationships between technical co-operation and foreign policy; Simon Rottenberg on how technology is transferred through private business firms; Arthur T. Mosher on technical co-operation activities in the field of agriculture; R. E. Buchanan on the role of university contracts in programs of technical co-operation; James G. Maddox and Howard R. Tolley on the training programs within technical co-operation; and Theodore W. Schultz on the distribution of technology and economic development.

These studies are the sole responsibility of the authors. They are building stones for the NPA Special Policy Committee in its efforts to resolve policy issues in the area of technical co-operation.

A major activity of the Special Policy Committee is to correlate the findings of the research staff and to prepare an over-all policy report on technical co-operation. Meanwhile, the committee is issuing recommendations or policy statements on matters which in its opinion warrant special attention. (The committee's reports to date have been published in a special series of NPA pamphlets.) In addition, the committee plans one or more case studies of particular programs as illustrations of a few of the problems which are common to many of the activities studied in the NPA project. A case study of ACAR's efforts to help stimulate better agricultural practices and rural living in Brazil was the first pamphlet of this type.

The NPA is grateful for the Ford Foundation's financial support and is deeply indebted to all who are contributing to this project: To the Special Policy Committee members; to the project's research staff; and to other individuals—too numerous to list—in Latin America and the United States, in the United Nations and its specialized agencies, and in the Organization of American States, for their invaluable co-operation and generosity with time and knowledge. Our special thanks go to Dr. James G. Maddox, research associate of the project, for his work on *Technical Assistance by Religious Agencies in Latin America,* and to the Special Policy Committee for its accompanying statement of policy issues and recommendations, which follows the report.

H. CHRISTIAN SONNE
Chairman, Board of Trustees

PREFACE

Knowledge is a powerful engine in achieving economic growth. There are a number of long-established channels and one important new one through which useful knowledge is carried from one country to another. Point 4 is new. Broadly defined, it takes in not only our United States programs of technical assistance, now called *technical co-operation*, but also similar programs of the United Nations and of its specialized agencies. In addition, for Latin America there is the technical assistance work of the Organization of American States.

When we set for ourselves the task of finding out how Point 4 has functioned in Latin America, it soon became apparent to us that the established channels were also of major importance as carriers of new techniques of production and of useful knowledge. The interplay between the universities of Latin America and of the United States represents one such channel for knowledge. The foundations, notably the long effective work of the Rockefeller Foundation in health and more recently in agriculture in Latin America, represent another. United States business firms are to be found everywhere in Latin America and probably represent the largest channel of all. Then there is the outstanding work in education and health, and also to some extent in agriculture, of the religious groups, which is the burden of this study.

Latin America with its twenty diverse countries has turned out to be an excellent place to observe the established channels and the new as carriers of knowledge and to observe how this knowledge is related to cultural change and economic development.

Dr. James G. Maddox was able to draw upon unusual riches in his own experiences in undertaking this study. The role of knowledge, including technical assistance, in cultural change and economic development was not new to him. In his graduate studies he concentrated on social and economic institutions. He did much of the thinking out of which the Farm Security Administration emerged, which was an important effort to help poor farmers in the United States achieve economic progress. Then as economist and associate chief of the renowned Bureau of Agricultural Economics he again concentrated on problems of economic growth within agriculture. Following this he joined the staff of Nelson A. Rockefeller's organization, American International Association for Economic and Social Development, and there set his mind to the task of helping that organization develop educational, health, and agricultural programs which it sponsored in Venezuela and Brazil. In doing so he acquired considerable firsthand knowledge of Latin America—its people and problems. He is now a member of the American Universities Field Staff.

We shall publish a series of major studies concentrating on the activities of universities, business, religious groups, and public agencies of technical co-operation as carriers of knowledge. This is the first.

THEODORE W. SCHULTZ
Director of Research

TABLE OF CONTENTS

INTRODUCTION

For more than a half-century, large numbers of churches and religious agencies in the United States have been sending missionaries to Latin America. The primary motive of this missionary movement has been to spread the doctrines of Christianity and in some instances to increase the membership of particular denominations. However, increasing numbers of the missionaries have been concerned with organizing and operating schools, hospitals, clinics, social service centers, and demonstration farms. These technical service activities are not only an important feature of the total missionary effort but also a significant expression of the willingness of the people of the United States to assist their Latin-American neighbors in raising their levels of living and increasing the productiveness of their enterprises.

The transfer of technical knowledge and skills from the United States to Latin America was put on a well-organized basis by the religious agencies long before the "Good Neighbor" policy was announced or government-financed technical co-operation programs were instituted. There is, however, much similarity between the technical service activities of the religious agencies and the newer technical co-operation programs of the United States, the United Nations, and the Organization of American States. The motivations and some of the principles of administration may be different, but the nature of the problems which arise and the content of many of the programs are about the same.

The purpose of this study is to characterize and evaluate the technical work of the religious agencies in such a way that it will be of value to the religious organizations, to those in government who are engaged in foreign technical co-operation programs, to private foundations and philanthropic organizations, and to the millions of citizens who finance both private and public programs of this character.

1

The principal emergent conclusions are abstracted from field work in seven Latin-American countries. This field work involved interviews with many missionaries, public officials, and private citizens. The technical activities of the following mission posts were reviewed at first hand:

BOLIVIA

1. Farm and Bible School near Lake Titicaca, about 50 miles from La Paz (Oregon Friends)
2. American Clinic (Pfeifer Hospital) in La Paz (Methodist church)
3. Adventists College of Bolivia, a primary and secondary boarding-school near Cochabamba (Seventh Day Adventist church)
4. American Institute, a primary and secondary school in Cochabamba (Methodist church)

BRAZIL

1. Mackenzie Institute, a large educational institution in the city of São Paulo, which gives work at the primary, secondary, technical, commercial, and uinversity levels of instruction (sponsored by the Presbyterian church and operated by an independent board)
2. Educational Division of the YWCA in Rio de Janeiro
3. Brazilian Adventists College, a primary and secondary boarding-school located on a large farm near São Paulo (Seventh Day Adventist church)
4. People's Central Institute, a large social welfare center in Rio de Janeiro (Methodist church)
5. Organization for Rehabilitation and Training (ORT) Vocational Center, a technical school for boys and girls in Rio de Janeiro (Brazilian Israel Society of the Organization for Rehabilitation Training)
6. Primary school for the children of English-speaking parents in São Paulo (Oblates of Mary Immaculate)
7. Rural Evangelical Institute, a rural mission post with a boarding-school for boys and girls and a farm and agricultural extension program, near Itapina in the state of Espírito Santo (Methodist church)
8. Primary school and clinic in one of the poorer sections of Rio de Janeiro (Immaculate Conception Province of the Order of Friars)
9. Izabela Hendrix College, a primary and secondary boarding-school for girls in Belo Horizonte (Methodist church)
10. Gammon Institute, an educational institution with primary and secondary boarding-schools for boys and girls, a practical school of agricul-

ture, and a college of agriculture at the university level at Lavras in the state of Minas Gerais (Presbyterian church)

CHILE

1. Agricultural extension program and demonstration farm near the city of Temuco (Methodist church)
2. El Vergel, a large rural mission post with farm, boarding-schools, clinic, and social center near Angol (Methodist church)
3. The Mother and Child Maternity Hospital in a workingman's section of Santiago (Presbyterian church)
4. Sweet Memorial Institute, a social service center and training school for Christian leaders in Santiago (Methodist church)
5. Baptist College, a primary and secondary boarding-school for boys and girls in Temuco (Baptist church)
6. Santiago College, a primary and secondary boarding-school for girls in Santiago (sponsored by Methodist church but operated as an independent institution)

ECUADOR

1. United Andean Indian Mission, a rural post with farm, primary school, and hospital near Tabacundo (operated jointly by the United Brethren, Presbyterian, and Evangelical and Reformed churches)
2. Rural Brethren Mission, a farm, school, and clinic near Quito (Church of the Brethren)

MEXICO

1. Colegio del Tepeyac, a primary, secondary, and preparatory school for boys in one of the suburbs of Mexico City (Benedictine Order)
2. Division of the Rural Church and Agriculture in Union Theological Seminary in Mexico City (Methodist church)
3. Girls Normal Institute, a primary, secondary, and normal school for girls in Puebla (Methodist church)
4. Latin-American Hospital and Nursing School in Puebla (Baptist church)
5. Sara Alarcón School, a primary and secondary boarding-school for girls in one of the suburbs of Mexico City (Methodist church)
6. Camp and Rural Reconstruction Center (Camohmila) of the YMCA in the village of Tepoztlan

7. "The Voice of the Home" radio program with headquarters in Mexico City (Seventh Day Adventist church)

NICARAGUA

1. Moravian College, a primary and secondary school for boys and girls in Bluefields (Moravian church)
2. St. Joe College, a primary and secondary school for boys in Bluefields (Christian Brothers)
3. Baptist College, a primary and secondary boarding-school for boys and girls in Managua (Baptist church)
4. Baptist Hospital and Nursing School in Managua (Baptist church)

PARAGUAY

1. International College, a primary and secondary school for boys and girls in Asunción (Disciples of Christ)
2. Clinic in Asunción (Seventh Day Adventist church)
3. Baptist Hospital in Asunción (Baptist church)
4. Primary school in Asunción (Redemptorist Order)

Much of the material describing the size of the missionary enterprise was obtained from letters and questionnaires sent to the religious agencies, as well as from published reports of mission boards and societies. The basic statistical material about the types of technical projects sponsored by the agencies was drawn from Department of State Publication No. 4422, *Guide to Technical Services of United States Voluntary Agencies Abroad.* Special studies and summaries issued by the director of the Missionary Research Library in New York City and by the Mission Secretariat in Washington, D.C., were also used.

Despite the care that has been taken in assembling the factual material, much remains to be desired in the way of statistical precision. The very nature of the missionary enterprise is such that its administrators place little emphasis on reports and quantitative measures of progress. Many of the statistical indexes used in the report are no more than rough approximations. However, the lack of statistical precision does not invalidate any of the major findings and conclusions.

Although this study is divided into five chapters, it is primarily concerned with three major topics. First, there is a brief description of some of the major characteristics of Latin-American society. This is presented in chapter 1, where it is intended to enhance the reader's understanding of the work of the religious agencies. Second, there is a description of the scope and nature of the technical services of the agencies, presented in chapters 2, 3, and 4. Third, there are conclusions about these activities and recommended ways of making them more effective. These are discussed in chapter 5.

The study has been made possible only through the excellent cooperation of a large number of missionary groups, both in the United States and in field stations. There is not room here to list the many people who have contributed, but the author is exceedingly grateful to all those who gave him information and insights into the work of United States religious agencies in Latin America. Particular acknowledgment should be made of the excellent help rendered by Dr. R. Pierce Beaver, director of the Missionary Research Library, and by the Rev. Frederick M. McGuire, executive secretary of the Mission Secretariat.

1 CULTURAL CHARACTERISTICS OF LATIN AMERICA

Latin America, which for the purposes of this report is defined as all of Central and South America, including Mexico and the Caribbean islands, is a large and complex region. In land area it is more than two and one-half times that of the United States. It is made up of twenty independent countries and a few territorial possessions of England, France, and Holland.[1] It is presently populated by about one hundred and sixty-five million people. Although it is predominantly a tropical region, there are large areas which, because of either altitude or latitude, have a temperate climate.

One finds great variations from area to area within the region in population characteristics, in the level of social and economic development, in the distribution of resources, and in social organization. In some areas in Latin America uncivilized savages roam the tropical forests, while, within two to three hundred miles, there are well-educated, sophisticated people living in modern cities. Within even shorter distances, it is possible to go from barren, snow-capped mountains to lush, tropical areas of rich land. It is not uncommon to find people who have traveled in Europe or the United States, who speak two or three languages, and who exemplify the most modern refinements of Western civilization, living in the same communities with descendants of the ancient Inca Indians, whose clothing, housing, daily forms of work, and language are little different from what they were five hundred years ago.

Even adjacent countries, with essentially the same climate, soil,

1. These possessions would have been completely excluded from consideration in this study, except for the fact that some of the statistics pertaining to missionary activity are available only for the West Indian islands as a group or for several Central American countries as a unit. These classifications of statistical data prevented the exclusion of the territorial possessions without at the same time eliminating data pertaining to countries that were originally settled and controlled by Spain. In no other manner, however, have the English, French, and Dutch possessions been considered.

6

and agricultural potentialities, have never utilized their resources in the same way or to the same degree. For instance, Haiti and the Dominican Republic share the same island, the drier and more rugged part being in Haiti, but the population density in the latter country is about 300 people per square mile while that in the Dominican Republic is 115. Likewise, El Salvador has almost eight times as many people per square mile as neighboring Nicaragua. Differences of this character, examples of which could be added by the score, suggest that the most serious problems of the region are "not with nature's gifts but with man's mentality." It is to the latter, of course, that the missionary enterprise is directed. And it is with the characteristics of the people—their levels of living, their social, economic, and political institutions—that this chapter is primarily concerned.

Racial and Cultural Inheritance

Present-day Latin America is part and parcel of Western culture. The casual traveler from the United States, particularly if he goes only to the larger cities of Latin America, will see things with which he is well acquainted. The predominant language is Spanish, except for Portuguese in Brazil and French in Haiti (and excluding Dutch and English, spoken in some of the Indies). The language may seem strange to the traveler from the United States, but most of the things that he will see, such as the clothes of the people, the houses in which they live, the architecture of the cities, the automobiles and horse-drawn vehicles, and even much of the food that he eats, will be similar to those to which he is accustomed. He will feel more at home in any Latin-American country than he would if he were in the Middle East or South Asia.

Even though Latin America is part of Western culture and in many outward appearances is similar to the United States, there are differences of great importance. Many of these come from a mixture of historical factors associated with the racial and cultural backgrounds of the present population.

There have been three great streams of racial influence on Latin America: (1) the original Indian population; (2) African Negroes, originally imported as slaves; and (3) the early settlers from Spain and Portugal. At the time of the Spanish conquest, there were highly developed Indian cultures in the highlands of what are now Mexico, Guatemala, Ecuador, Peru, and Bolivia. It is in these countries that the Indian influence is strongest today. However, there were numerous Indian tribes, in various stages of civilization, throughout most of the region. As settlement advanced and plantation farming developed, large numbers of African slaves were brought into the West Indies, eastern Brazil, and the coastal areas of several countries bordering the Caribbean. They have had an important influence on the racial composition in these parts of Latin America.

To a far greater degree than the northern Europeans who settled the United States and Canada, the Spanish and Portuguese intermixed with the native Indians and later with the African Negroes. After the Latin-American colonies gained their freedom, there was a considerable influx of Italians and Germans into several of the countries. In some places in Latin America, there are also a few orientals. To one viewing the region as a whole, the Indian, the Negro, the white, and the mixture of white and Indian called "mestizo" are the predominant racial types, with the exception of the Caribbean area, where the mulatto dominates.

Although there are few quantitative indexes of the racial composition of the Latin-American population, the following classification of countries, according to the predominance of racial type,[2] gives a rough idea of the situation at the present time:

Countries with Indian predominance: Bolivia, Ecuador, Guatemala, Mexico, Paraguay, and Peru

Countries with white predominance: Argentina, Chile, Costa Rica, and Uruguay

Countries with Negro predominance: Cuba, Haiti, and Dominican Republic

Countries with mestizo predominance: Colombia, El Salvador, Honduras, Nicaragua, and Venezuela

Countries with great racial mixtures: Brazil and Panama

2. The classification of countries by predominance of racial type was suggested to the author by Aníbal Buitrón, chief of the Section of Labor, Migration, and Social Security in the Pan American Union; see also Wilbert E. Moore, *Industrialization and Labor* (Ithaca: Cornell University Press, 1951), Table 1, p. 207.

As compared with the United States, there is little racial discrimination in Latin America, but differences between economic and social classes are sometimes extreme. It is not easy to find a close correlation between racial type, on the one hand, and economic and social status, on the other, but there is a higher-than-average concentration of white people in the upper classes. However, one can find exceptions to this generalization.

The Spanish and Portuguese, like the English, French, and Dutch, tried to transplant to the New World many of the political, social, economic, and religious institutions of their homelands. Some of these have been influential in shaping the course of Latin America's development, and a few of them are still important. Fifteenth- and sixteenth-century Spain was a country with many large landed estates owned by a few families and worked by poverty-stricken peasants. There was often a feudalistic relationship between the owners of these estates and the people who worked them. The former were semiautonomous political chiefs, who could both make the local laws governing their peasants and dispense justice under them. Spain was also a military country. The Moors were finally driven out in 1492, the year that Columbus discovered the New World. The end of the Moorish wars left large numbers of unemployed soldiers, many of whom claimed noble blood and wanted to maintain their social positions by continuing in the army. They were among some of the first migrants to what is now Latin America. Finally, Spain was ardently Catholic. The Catholic faith had been one of the main unifying forces in the long fight against the Moors and was viewed as the faith to be carried to the colonies.

The plantation system of agriculture, with feudalistic tenure relationships, a strong military class with important political power, highly centralized government, and Catholic tenets, with the church having close ties to the state, were four institutions imported from sixteenth-century Spain which have had great influence in shaping the broad outlines of Latin-American society. These institutions have undergone significant changes over the last four centuries and have lost much of their original force, particularly in such countries as Mexico, Uruguay, and Costa Rica. Nevertheless, the large landowner, the army officer, and the Catholic priest are still important influences in most of the Latin-American countries. They, along with a growing group of well-to-do industrial and commercial families, tend to constitute an elite class, the size and strength of which varies from country to country but which usually exercises significant political power and often sets the norms of opinion with respect to many types of economic and social relations.

Many social characteristics of Latin America appear to be of the same general type as those commonly attributed to the aristocratic culture of Europe before the Industrial Revolution and which also characterized the "Old South" of the United States. For instance, one observes that many academic men in Latin America are loath to work with their hands. They seem to feel that they will lose social status if they "teach by doing." Consequently, they rarely go outside the classroom or laboratory to engage in demonstration work in the field. Likewise, some of them shun empirical investigations and show little interest in devising ways and means of applying science to the day-to-day problems of living. In some of the countries, the man of letters, the lawyer, the politician, and the army officer appear to have a higher social standing than the scientist, the industrialist, or the businessman. Furthermore, the curriculums of many Latin-American educational institutions emphasize language, rhetoric, mathematics, logic, and moral philosophy but put relatively less weight on science, engineering, agriculture, economics, and sociology.

Two broad streams of thought that have been important in shaping the culture of most of western Europe and of the United States were of relatively little significance in Latin America until the colonies gained their independence from Spain and Portugal: (1) the growth of scientific methods of investigation and the widespread application of science to the problems of agriculture, industry, and transportation and (2) the moral and political ideas associated with the concept of "equality of rights" among men. Spain and Portugal had largely escaped the direct impact of such important social movements as the Reformation, the Industrial Revolution, and the rise of laissez faire capitalism. After the Latin-American colonies gained their independence (1820–25) many new influences began to be felt, particularly from France, England, and the United States. Political, social, and economic institutions from these countries have had significant impacts in many parts of Latin America for more than a century. There are, however, still many cultural traits of the early inheritance from the colonial period.

Social and Political Features

One of the characteristics of Latin-American culture which most often impresses North Americans is the wide gap between the upper and lower classes in society and the relatively small number of people of middle-class status. The class structure of the region varies considerably from country to country, but in most areas there is a small class of educated, wealthy people, many of whom have traveled widely and most of whom live quite comfortably at the top of the social hierarchy. At the other extreme is a much larger group of exceedingly poor people, who have little, if any, education; whose food, clothing, and housing are meager; and who often appear to have few prospects of improving their condition. In between these extremes there is a growing middle class in most of the countries, whose members have come largely from lower-class ranks. The middle class is smaller than in the United States, but it includes many of the same kinds of people—small shopkeepers, teachers, a few lawyers, dentists and doctors, white-collar workers in commercial and industrial concerns, and people engaged in various types of service trades.

Traditionally, upper-class status was limited in most of the countries to families with large landholdings. With the rapid growth of cities and the consequent rise of business and professional groups, a few wealthy but landless families have achieved upper-class status. Nevertheless, in most of the countries there is still a strong tendency for wealthy families to invest rather heavily in land, although it is now quite common to find upper-class families with substantial investments in industry, commerce, and banking, as well as in land. In Mexico and more recently in Bolivia, land-reform laws have been effective in breaking up many of the old landed estates.

The lower classes make up the great majority of the Latin-American population. Most of the people are laborers or small sharecropping tenants on large farms, with almost no education and few prospects of becoming independent operators. An increasing number, but still a small proportion of the total, are industrial and service workers around the cities. In countries like Guatemala, Ecuador, Peru, and Bolivia, where the original Indian population was large at the time of the conquest, the Indian usually ranks at the very bottom of the social scale. Some of them are hardly more than beasts of burden—doing the work of oxen and donkeys. On the other hand, some of the Indians have important handicraft enterprises, such as weaving and pottery-making, which put them in the class of skilled workers. Even in these cases, however, they are more or less social and political outcasts.

In the great lower-class population, there is tremendous waste of human resources in the form of a short life-span, ill-health, malnutrition, illiteracy, and lack of incentives. The door of opportunity, though never completely closed, is so narrowly open to most people of lower-class rank that many of them have little hope for significant improvement. Particularly in rural areas, they continue their plodding tasks from generation to generation, following in the footsteps of their forefathers in an incessant struggle to get their hands on enough food and clothing to keep body and soul together. In urban areas the level of living of the lower classes is usually somewhat better, though thousands live in slums where housing and sanitary conditions are unbelievably bad. It appears to be around the cities, however, that people of lower-class rank can most effectively climb the social and economic ladder to middle-class status. Moreover, the growth of industry around quite a few of the Latin-American cities is providing jobs for many illiterate countrypeople who a few decades ago had almost no opportunity outside their native rural communities. The building of roads is also doing much to put isolated rural villages in contact with the outside world and to open up new vistas to the people, as well as new markets for both urban and rural products.

Following the wars for independence, when most of the population was agricultural; when agricultural society was organized along aristocratic lines, with strong elements of feudalism governing the relations between landowner and worker; when the new ruling classes had had no experience in self-government and were acquainted only with the operations of a monarchy and a highly centralized colonial administration, most of the Latin-American countries adopted a republican form of government. Indeed, some of their constitutions were modeled rather closely on that of the United States. They were sometimes written by political idealists, who had been fired with enthusiasm by the writings of the French radicals and strongly influenced by the works of such North Americans as Jefferson and Paine.

During the colonial period, there had been no real separation of powers in government. Officials of the colonial administration, from the viceroys to those with only local responsibilities, had enjoyed both political and military authority. They had been able to issue orders that had the force of law and had also acted as judges. It was difficult for the new ruling groups to understand the concept of a president, congress, and courts, acting independently in their respective spheres of responsibility. When authority was further divided between federal and state governments, as was provided by some of the constitutions, the problem was multiplied in complexity. Many of the new leaders were military men who had risen to fame during the wars for independence. They usually had little understanding of political processes and were often lacking in the degree of forbearance that was necessary to nurture and guide the budding democracies.

As a consequence of the many factors that were unfavorable to the development of republican and democratic forms of government, political power often fell into the hands of men who could command the support of the army. Many decisions could not be made and enforced without resort to the military establishments and the men who commanded the armed forces. Several of the countries were beset by civil wars, some of which resulted in much bloodshed and severe disruptions of production and trade. In country after country, power became concentrated in the hands of the executive; the legislative and judicial branches of government were pushed into the background, and political campaigns often degenerated into internecine struggles between "strong men" vying for control of the national power. Political parties were often organized to support or oppose a man, not to define issues.

Although much of the political history of Latin America during the past century and a quarter could be written in terms of a struggle between those forces and elements in society which were supporting democratic processes and procedures and those that favored "one-man" rule, with the strong-arm practices and reliance on military power which usually go with the latter, it cannot be said that the issue has been finally resolved. Dictatorships and government by small cliques still exist in several of the Latin-American countries. In others, however, "government by consent of the governed" appears to have won out.

With a few important exceptions, it is generally the upper-class groups that control political power. Usually they have the support of the army. In some cases it is a representative of the army who holds the reins, and he, in turn, has the support of a considerable segment, if not all, of the upper classes. Governmental operations are commonly highly centralized. Brazil, Argentina, Venezuela, and Mexico have federal systems, but in recent years it is only in the first and last of these that there has been any real distribution of power between federal and state governments. Moreover, in most of the countries governmental employees below cabinet rank customarily have little authority to make decisions, and in some of the countries even cabinet members have to refer relatively minor questions to the chief executive. Local citizens rarely get practice and experience in governing themselves, even with respect to such questions as the operation of primary schools, the construction and maintenance of farm-to-market roads, or the selection of municipal officials.

The Economy and Levels of Living

Although the social and political organization of many of the Latin-American countries gives heavy weight to conservative, upper-class values and, in some instances, still has elements of feudalism in it, the region as a whole is growing and developing. Population is increasing at a rate of about 2.3 per cent per year, which apparently is higher than any other comparably large area of the world. In most of the countries large numbers of people are moving to the cities; means of transportation are increasing; in several areas, manufacturing is expanding; and technology is improving, slowly in most places but rapidly in some. These and related forces are breaking down old social forms and institutions. Rapid change is the order of the day in most Latin-American countries.

One of the significant trends within the area is the expansion of industry, transportation, and commerce. An index of this is provided by estimates of the Economic Commission for Latin America of the United Nations, which show that the annual average rate of increase in the agricultural labor force between 1945 and 1953 was only 1.6 per cent, whereas it was over 2.0 per cent in all other sectors of the economy, and was 3.3 per cent in manufacturing and the building trades. Likewise, the total output from agriculture did not grow so rapidly during the same period as did output in other sectors of the economy. In other words, agriculture was expanding, but not so rapidly as manufacturing, construction, transportation, and commerce.[3]

Although there are various indications that the region as a whole is making considerable progress toward developing the non-farm sectors of the economy—the growth of industry has been very rapid in recent years in certain areas, such as São Paulo (Brazil), Caracas (Venezuela), and Mexico City (Mexico)—it is nevertheless true that Latin America is still predominantly an agricultural area. In 1953 about 58 per cent of the active population was engaged in agriculture, and only 42 per cent in other types of activity. A large share of the manufacturing and commercial activities was concerned with processing and distributing agricultural commodities or with supplying goods and services to farm people. Moreover, the export of agricultural products usually accounts for about half the total value of exports from the region, and most Latin-American countries are still heavily dependent on imports for many manufactured consumer goods, as well as for heavy equipment and machinery, most of which has to be paid for by the export of agricultural commodities and minerals. The latter ordinarily represent about one-fourth the value of the region's exports.[4]

It is difficult to make useful quantitative comparisons of the levels of living of the people in Latin America with those in the United States or other areas of the world, partly because their habits of consumption are different, partly because there is great variation from one area to another within Latin America, and partly because

3. The data are from the *Economic Survey of Latin America, 1953,* prepared by the Secretariat of the Economic Commission for Latin America, Department of Economic Affairs, United Nations.

4. *Ibid.*

the data for many indexes of welfare either are not available or are not comparable from country to country. Notwithstanding the difficulties of measurement, Latin America as a whole stands out as a part of Western culture in which poverty is common. When judged by North American standards, a great proportion of the Latin-American people are desperately poor. In all the countries a small upper class lives very well, some members quite lavishly. In most of the countries many middle-class people live comfortably, and in the larger cities a significant proportion of them live about as well as ordinary white-collar workers in the United States. Moreover, in such places as Argentina, Uruguay, southern Brazil, Venezuela, and parts of Mexico and Chile the average level of living is several times higher than in such countries as Haiti, Ecuador, Bolivia, and El Salvador. There are areas in the better-developed countries of Latin America where the majority of the people live as well as, or perhaps better than, those in the more backward parts of southern United States. But in most of the countries most of the people live quite poorly.

Among the great mass of the working population, but particularly in rural areas, life-expectancy is considerably shorter than in the United States; infant mortality rates are two to three times as high; housing is usually of poor quality, and overcrowding is common; the number of available doctors and dentists per thousand people is low; ill-health, poor nutrition, and illiteracy are widespread. Thousands of families go through life without ever being attended by a physician, though such diseases as tuberculosis, influenza-pneumonia, and diarrhea-enteritis are common. Hundreds of thousands of children never set foot in a schoolroom, and many more never get beyond the third or fourth grade.

Most of the countries are trying to improve conditions of life for the poorer people, but back of the grinding poverty is an economic system which is a low producer of goods and services. Although a small upper class often obtains a relatively large share of the total output, the real economic problem of the region is low productivity per worker. There is simply not enough produced for everyone to live well, regardless of how it is distributed.

This low productivity stems from a multitude of factors, among which are a shortage of capital, heavy reliance on antiquated technology, and a working population which suffers from handicaps of poor training and in some cases from ill-health and undernourishment, as well as a lack of incentives. Moreover, Latin America is no El Dorado of natural resources. It is desperately short of coal—the basic fuel for an industrial economy. Its areas of fertile soil are probably less extensive in relation to its total land than is the case in either Europe or the United States. Its forests have a low proportion of softwoods—the type of timber most commonly used for construction purposes—and the great mixture of species on a given area of land which characterizes most tropical forests makes the economic utilization of many of its timber resources difficult and expensive. Finally, many of its good land areas and much of its timber are located at great distances from markets and centers of population.

Though capital shortages, backward technologies, an inefficient labor force, inadequate natural resources, and difficulties of transportation are real and important impediments to rapid increases in productivity, one cannot escape the conclusion that much progress could be made by improving the management of many private business firms; by greater efficiencies in the administration of government; by widespread education for both adults and children; and by numerous changes in social, political, and economic processes aimed at providing greater incentives to lower-class people. In short, the better organization of human resources in Latin-American society offers great opportunities for improving the wealth and well-being of the region. It is in these areas of activity that the work of religious groups is significant.

Within a half-century after the wars of independence, United States missionaries were at work in Latin America. Much of the early effort, as is true even today, was concerned exclusively with word-of-mouth preaching. By the beginning of the twentieth century, however, the missionary movement had already turned to organizing and financing schools, in which the dissemination of Christian dogma was secondary to the teaching of reading, writing, and arithmetic. Between the two world wars there was a rapid growth of schools, hospitals, and demonstration farms sponsored by religious groups.

Today there is fairly general recognition that the promulgation of Christianity cannot be limited exclusively to preaching. Leading

theologians agree that a wide area of social service activity is a necessary part of church responsibility. Most denominations will insist
that "the source of these social services must always be the redeem-
ing Gospel, never mere humanitarianism." That salvation is in
Christ, not in modern techniques and technology, is a point emphasized by Protestants and Catholics alike. There are doctrinal differences, but most modern-minded church leaders will agree that "the
fruits of creation and redemption must be used and enjoyed by the
integral man. The work of the missioner cannot be one-sided."[5]

5. Msgr. L. G. Ligutti, *Rural Missions*, No. 85 (winter, 1953).

2 SCOPE OF MISSIONARY ACTIVITY

Slightly more than 300 United States religious agencies have sent missionaries abroad during recent years. The total number of foreign missionaries serving under the auspices of these agencies is over 22,000. However, only about 175 agencies have been sending missionaries to Latin America, of which between 90 and 95 are Protestant organizations and most of the rest are Catholic. Collectively, these agencies have one or more missionaries in every Latin-American country and in most of the neighboring British, French, and Dutch possessions. The total number of their missionaries in Latin America was about 5,300 in 1952, of whom approximately three-fourths were Protestants and one-fourth Catholic (Table 1). Most of this missionary activity, however, was carried on by relatively few organizations. About 12 Protestant agencies plus 3 Catholic institutes had well over 50 per cent of the total United States missionaries working in Latin America.[1]

Representatives of religious groups from the United States do not account for all the missionaries in Latin America. There are many Catholic priests from European countries, particularly from Spain, Portugal, Italy, and France. Although the vast majority of church members in Latin America are of the Catholic faith, several of the countries have a shortage of native priests and thus have come to rely heavily on European countries for their clergy.

Because of limited resources, this study is concerned only with

1. The data in this paragraph have come from the files and reports of the Missionary Research Library, Union Theological Seminary, New York City, and from *U.S. Catholic Missionary Personnel Overseas in 1951* (Washington, D.C.: Mission Secretariat).

It is recognized that the representatives of some of the agencies, such as American Friends Service Committee, YMCA, YWCA, American ORT Federation, and perhaps others, do not think of themselves as "missionaries." There seems to be, however, no better single term by which to designate the representatives of the many different types of religious-based agencies. Since the term is applicable in the great majority of cases, it is used throughout this study to include the foreign personnel of all types of religious agencies.

the technical work of religious agencies with headquarters in the United States or staffed with United States personnel. The proportion that such groups represent of all foreign missionaries in Latin America is not known, but it certainly falls considerably short of the total.

TABLE 1

U S. PROTESTANT AND CATHOLIC MISSIONARIES IN LATIN-AMERICAN COUNTRIES IN RELATION TO POPULATION

COUNTRY	POPULATION* IN 1952 (000 OMITTED)	NUMBER OF MISSIONARIES			
		Protestant 1952†	Catholic 1951‡	Total	Per 100,000 People
Argentina	18,056	162	20	182	1.01
Bolivia	3,089	252	70	322	10.42
Brazil	54,477	749	249	998	1.83
Chile	5,932	142	101	243	4.10
Colombia	11,768	294	8	302	2.57
Cuba	5,469§	53	8	61	1.12
Ecuador	3,350	220	0	220	6.57
Haiti	3,200	2	29	31	0.97
Mexico	26,922	480	37	517	1.92
Paraguay	1,464	53	16	69	4.71
Peru	8,864	257	84	341	3 85
Uruguay	2,353‖	71	1	72	3.06
Venezuela	5,280	248	10	258	4.89
Central America#	9,168	431	243	674	7.35
West Indies**	5,717	509	483	992	17.35
Total	165,109	3,923	1,359	5,282	3.20

* United Nations, *Statistical Yearbook 1953.*
† Unpublished data from Missionary Research Library, New York.
‡ *U.S. Catholic Missionary Personnel Overseas in 1951* (Washington, D.C.: Mission Secretariat).
§ 1951.
‖ 1949.
Not including Mexico. The data for Guatemala and Nicaragua included in the total were for 1951.
** Not including Cuba and Haiti. Data for a few of the minor islands included in the total were for years earlier than 1952.

There is about one missionary from the United States per 30,000 people in Latin America. As shown in Table 1, however, there is great variation among the countries with respect to the concentration of missionary activity. Brazil, for instance, has the largest number of United States missionaries, but it is such a big country that there are less than two missionaries per 100,000 people. The heaviest concentration, relative to population, is (1) in the West Indies, exclusive of Cuba and Haiti; (2) in Bolivia; (3) in the Central American countries south of Mexico; and (4) in Ecuador. There

may be some slight tendency for the number of missionaries relative to population to be heaviest in the poorly developed countries;
however, there are some notable exceptions. Haiti, for example,
which is one of the most poverty-stricken countries in Latin America, has the lowest number of missionaries from the United States
per 100,000 people, whereas Chile, one of the better-developed
countries, has a higher concentration relative to its population than
either Paraguay or Peru (Table 1).

Protestant missionaries from the United States outnumber the
Catholics almost three to one. However, it is probable that the emphasis which each group is giving to Latin America relative to
other overseas areas is about the same. For instance, sample studies
of the major Protestant agencies indicate that about 27 per cent of
all their foreign missionaries were stationed in Latin America in
1952.[2] And the 1,359 Catholic missionaries from the United States
who were in Latin America in 1951 represented approximately 30
per cent of the total number in overseas posts.[3]

Technical Service Work

The number and geographic distribution of missionaries in Latin
America do not, unfortunately, give us a clear picture of what religious agencies are doing in the way of technical activities.

Representatives of some Protestant denominations do little more
than "street-corner preaching" and disseminating religious literature. This is particularly true of fundamentalist and pentecostal
groups. Likewise, a significant proportion of Catholic priests sent to
Latin America from the United States concern themselves almost
exclusively with spiritual guidance and a rather narrow range of
church functions. On the other hand, there are numerous Protestant
denominations and many individual Catholic priests and nuns who
work part time in various types of social service or technical service
work, such as teaching, ministering to the sick, organizing recreational programs, and conducting adult-education classes. Still others
operate schools, hospitals, and farms—types of activity not directly
related to evangelism. There is, therefore, in the total picture of

2. From unpublished data supplied by R. Pierce Beaver, director, Missionary
Research Library.

3. From Table 1 and *U.S. Catholic Missionary Personnel Overseas in 1951.*

missionary activity everything from itinerant preaching to the operation of well-established institutions which are concerned primarily
with problems of education and health—from nineteenth-century,
frontier-type evangelism to the management of modern centers of
science.

A sample study of the primary responsibilities of almost 3,000
Protestant missionaries, representing 84 different United States religious agencies in Latin America in 1952, gives the distribution
shown in Table 2.[4] The major part of the missionary effort among

TABLE 2

	Per Cent
General churchworkers and evangelists	66
Educational workers	24
Nurses and medical technicians	5
Industrial and technical workers	2
Doctors and dentists	1
Agricultural workers	1
Social service workers	1

Protestant groups in Latin America is devoted to churchwork and
evangelism. Only one-third of the missionaries were engaged primarily in types of activity that might reasonably be defined as
"technical service work." Some of the general workers and evangelists give a part of their time to educational activities. The exact proportion, however, is difficult to estimate.

Another indication of the volume of technical work on the part of
religious agencies can be obtained from the Department of State
Publication No. 4422, *Guide to Technical Services of United States
Voluntary Agencies Abroad.* It lists 48 United States religious
agencies that had active projects in Latin America, between 1949
and 1951, in the fields of education, health, agriculture, social
service, and industry (Table 3). The listing is not entirely complete.
Through field studies and a review of the annual reports and publications of missionary organizations, additional agencies have been
added to the list, bringing it up to 66 agencies known to have

4. Unpublished data from the files of the Missionary Research Library. Similar figures are not available for Catholic missionaries. However, general ob-
servations in the seven Latin-American countries where field work was done
suggests that Catholic missionaries from the United States probably do slightly
less in the way of social service or technical assistance work than does the average
Protestant.

TABLE 3

PROTESTANT

1. American Baptist Convention
2. American Board of Commissioners for Foreign Missions
3. American Friends Board of Missions
4. American Friends Service Committee
5. Board for Christian Work in Santo Domingo
6. Brethren Service Commission
7. Central American Mission
8. California Yearly Meeting of Friends°
9. Christian and Missionary Alliance
10. Church of God
11. Church of the Nazarene
12. Congregational Christian Service Committee
13. Cumberland Presbyterian Church
14. Disciples of Christ
15. Evangelical Mission Covenant Church of America°
16. Evangelical United Brethren Church°
17. Evangelical and Reformed Church
18. Free Methodist Church of North America
19. Gospel Missionary Union°
20. Latin American Mission
21. Mennonite Central Committee
22. The Methodist Church
23. Moravian Church in America
24. Oregon Yearly Meeting of Friends°
25. Presbyterian Church in the United States of America
26. Presbyterian Church in the United States
27. Protestant Episcopal Church
28. Seventh Day Adventist General Conference
29. Seventh Day Baptist Missionary Society°
30. Southern Baptist Convention
31. Unevangelized Fields Mission
32. Unitarian Service Committee
33. United Andean Indian Mission
34. United Brethren in Christ
35. United Lutheran Church
36. World Mission Prayer League°
37. Wesleyan Methodist Missionary Society°
38. West Indies Mission, Inc.
39. Young Men's Christian Association
40. Young Women's Christian Association

* All agencies with an asterisk (*) following their names have been added, on the basis of information obtained from field work or from annual reports and publications of missionary-sending agencies, to those listed in *Guide to Technical Services of United States Voluntary Agencies Abroad.*

TABLE 3—*Continued*

ROMAN CATHOLIC†

1. Augustinians
2. Benedictines*
3. Capuchins
4. Christian Brothers*
5. Congregation of the Holy Cross*
6. Congregation of St. Agnes*
7. Daughters of Wisdom*
8. Dominican Sisters
9. Franciscans
10. Jesuits
11. Little Company of Mary
12. Marinists
13. Maryknoll Missioners
14. Maryknoll Sisters
15. Oblates of Mary Immaculate
16. Redemptorists*
17. Sister Adorers of the Most Precious Blood*
18. Sisters of Charity
19. Sisters of the Holy Cross*
20. Sisters of Mercy
21. Sisters of the Immaculate Heart of Mary
22. Society of the Precious Blood*
23. Ursuline Nuns
24. Vincentians*

OTHER

1. American ORT Federation
2. Church of the Latter Day Saints

† Many of the Roman Catholic agencies are international organizations. Those included in this table have technical assistance projects in Latin America that are directed by United States personnel. There are at least thirteen additional Catholic agencies of this type with one or more North Americans among their workers. It is not known, however, that they are engaged in technical assistance activities. Of this number, nine are communities of nuns, who can be presumed to be working in schools, hospitals, or other social service activities.

technical assistance projects. They represent approximately 38 per cent of the total number of United States religious agencies that are sending missionaries to Latin America.

It is significant that at least one-third of the U.S. missionaries in Latin America are primarily engaged in technical service work and that about 38 per cent of the agencies operating in Latin America have technical projects. These are two distinctly different measures of the extent to which religious agencies engage in technical service activities in Latin America. Both indexes may be a little low. Some evangelists and churchworkers perform part-time work in the field of general education. Likewise, there may be a slight undercounting of agencies with technical projects. The errors, however, are not large.

If we conclude that 40 per cent of the missionary effort in Latin America is primarily concerned with such activities as general education, health, agriculture, and social service programs, we shall be essentially correct. This suggests that the equivalent of approximately 2,100 United States missionaries are engaged full time in these types of activities.[5]

Although it is difficult to estimate the amount of money that United States religious agencies send to Latin America, there are rough indications that it may be $20,000,000–$25,000,000 per year. If such a figure is approximately correct and if about 40 per cent of it is used in the fields of education, health, agriculture, and social services, the religious agencies are administering a technical program in Latin America which involves contributions from the United States of $8,000,000–$10,000,000 per year. These contributions, though highly significant from many points of view, are a poor indication of the scope of the work being done. Many of the schools, hospitals, clinics, and farms operated by the missionaries are almost wholly self-supporting. A large proportion of the contributions from the United States is used to pay the salaries and expenses of the missionaries stationed in Latin America and to enlarge or improve the physical facilities of the mission posts. Moreover, some of the schools and hospitals receive substantial donations from local citizens, and in some of the countries the governments supply a part of the funds needed to operate the schools and hospitals directed by the missionaries. This is quite a common practice in the case of activities operated by Catholic missionaries. Some Protestant groups are loath to accept funds from governments of predominantly Catholic countries, and there is sufficient feeling against Protestants in some of the countries that funds from government sources are not available to them. There are numerous cases, however, of schools managed by Protestant missionaries which receive funds from governments.

In view of the various sources of income to many of the missionary activities, it is almost certain that the contributions from the

5. Forty per cent of the 5,282 missionaries shown in Table 1 equals 2,113.

United States represent a small proportion of the total operating funds that flow through the treasuries of the mission posts. Moreover, it must not be forgotten that if one were attempting to measure the scope of the technical services being carried forward in Latin America by all types of religious agencies, attention would have to be given to the activities of European missionaries. Among the most important of these are the Silesian Fathers, who for many years have operated numerous vocational and agricultural schools in various Latin-American countries. No attempt has been made in this study to take account of their efforts.

Clearly, however, the work of the United States agencies alone constitutes a major avenue for the flow of technical knowledge to Latin America. A group of 66 different agencies, with a field staff equivalent to about 2,100 full-time people, and involving annual contributions from the United States of $8,000,000–$10,000,000 for technical activities is a sizable effort. Although the work which the missionaries do is quite different from that of the technical assistance agencies of the United States government, it is not amiss to point out that there were only 664 technicians employed for work in Latin America by the government, at the end of June, 1954, and that its financial contribution to the technical co-operation program in Latin America, during the fiscal year 1954, was about $22,000,000. Thus, in terms of manpower, the activities of the religious groups are over three times as large as the government effort and almost half as large when measured in terms of dollar contributions from the United States.

3 TYPES OF TECHNICAL ACTIVITIES

The technical service work of United States religious agencies is plainly of significant size. Much of it has been under way for several decades. On what kinds of problems does it focus attention? What are its aims and methods? What is the relative emphasis given to different types of projects?

Apart from general churchwork and evangelism, the religious agencies have placed major emphasis on education. The 66 religious agencies listed in Table 3, each of which has one or more technical service projects in Latin America, are collectively sponsoring over 1,600 projects, of which more than 1,300 are schools. Healthwork ranks second, with 119 hospitals, clinics, and nursing schools. Agricultural programs take third place, with 43 projects. The distribution of these activities by type is given in Table 4.[1]

TABLE 4

Educational projects, not including nursing schools		1,363
Primary schools	1,070	
Secondary schools	145	
Commercial and vocational schools	58	
Unidentified schools	90	
Hospitals and clinics*		119
Farms and agricultural extension programs		43
Miscellaneous types of projects		94
Total projects		1,619

* Several of the hospitals also have nursing schools.

The religious agencies, by centering attention in the fields of education, health, and agriculture, pioneered in areas of activity that later became the focal points for the publicly financed programs administered by the Institute of Inter-American Affairs. With the latter agency, however, the order of emphasis in recent years

1. Arranged from information in Department of State Publication No. 4422, supplemented by field work and data from the Missionary Research Library and the Mission Secretariat.

has been first to agriculture, second to health, and third to education, when measured in terms of expenditures.

The number of projects of the religious agencies should not be confused with the number of mission stations or institutions. For instance, a common type of Protestant mission station in rural areas is a farm, on which are located a clinic or small hospital, a school for all primary grades and one or two secondary grades, and a church or chapel for religious services. Such a station is considered, in this study, to have four technical assistance projects—one in agriculture, one in health, and two in education, the last being a primary and a secondary school. A station of this type may also sponsor from one to twenty or thirty primary schools in the surrounding area, each of which we consider a separate project.

In urban centers, mission stations tend to be more specialized in function. Hospitals and schools, for instance, are rarely at the same site or under the same local management. A common urban health unit is a hospital, at which there are several outpatient clinics each week and a nursing school. A unit of this type has been counted as one project. A typical pattern among Catholic missionaries is for several priests to live together in a rectory, each being assigned a neighboring parish, in which he is responsible for all church functions and for general supervision of one or two parochial schools. Quite often the schools will be staffed partly by nuns from the United States. In a part of the rectory or in one of the school buildings there may be a clinic or treatment-room staffed by one or more nuns, who work under the general direction of a local public health doctor. In a situation of this type each of the schools and the clinic are considered to be separate technical projects.

Thus there is wide variety in the physical characteristics of mission stations. Of more importance are the activities or projects carried out in connection with them. These can be most readily understood in terms of a few major categories, which we shall take up in turn.

Educational Activities

The educational activities not of a strictly religious character are focused around primary and secondary schools, with a few specialized commercial and vocational schools. In practically all places where there is a secondary school, there are also one or more primary schools. Moreover, many of the commercial schools are, in reality, specialized departments of large secondary schools.

Collectively, the religious agencies of the United States have sponsored primary schools in every country of Latin America, secondary schools in most of them, and some type of commercial or

TABLE 5

NUMBER OF SCHOOLS SPONSORED BY UNITED STATES RELIGIOUS
AGENCIES IN LATIN AMERICA*

Country	Primary	Secondary	Technical†	Unidentified	Total
Argentina........	23	3	3	9	38
Bolivia..........	99	5	1	3	108
Brazil...........	245	41	16	16	318
Chile...........	70	11	6	....	87
Colombia........	37	10	1	8	56
Costa Rica......	14	....	1	1	16
Cuba...........	49	19	5	11	84
Dominican Republic	22	3	....	1	26
Ecuador........	12	4	....	....	16
El Salvador......	4	2	2	....	8
Guatemala......	19	2	4	3	28
Haiti...........	126	3	1	1	131
Honduras.......	10	2	....	6	18
Mexico..........	47	14	5	14	80
Nicaragua.......	24	5	1	1	31
Panama........	21	2	1	1	25
Paraguay........	11	1	....	....	12
Peru...........	160	8	4	1	173
Uruguay........	10	1	2	....	13
Venezuela......	13	2	1	....	16
British possessions	54	7	4	14	79
Total.......	1,070	145	58	90	1,363

* Arranged from information in the sources used for Table 4.
† Commercial-vocational schools.

vocational school in every country except four (Table 5). There are a few institutions offering work at the university level, but these are not numerous. Brazil, Peru, Haiti, and Bolivia all have more than 100 schools sponsored by United States religious agencies. El Salvador, with only 8 such schools, ranks lowest (Table 5).

Of the 1,363 schools (see Table 4), 1,157 are sponsored by Protestant agencies, 198 by Catholic, and the remaining 8 by other agencies. Four Protestant agencies, namely, the Seventh Day Adventist General Conference, the Methodist church, the Presbyterian

Church in the United States of America, and the Southern Baptist Convention, account for 876 of the schools, or 64 per cent of the total.

By almost any reasonable criteria, the primary school is the most important type of project of the religious agencies in Latin America. More agencies sponsor them than any other type of technical project; they far outnumber all others combined; and they touch the lives of more Latin-Americans than any other, unless it be the health clinics, in some of which large numbers of people receive simple treatments and inoculations. In contrast to the clinic, however, the primary school is likely to leave a lasting impression on many young people. Second only to the home, it can be a most potent force in shaping human personality, both by teaching the ordinary skills of reading, writing, and arithmetic and by instilling ideals and values.

The heavy emphasis which United States missionaries have placed on primary schools appears to be the result of three different factors. First and most important, it is a manifestation of the generally accepted view in the United States that elementary education should be universal—that all children should have access to primary schools. This idea of universal education has not been a commonly accepted goal of the Latin-American culture. Neither governments nor indigenous religious institutions have been committed to the principle of providing educational facilities for all children. True, there has been in recent years a growing recognition that educational opportunities should be widened. But neither the goal of a primary education for all children nor especially the implementing principles by which to achieve such an objective are common characteristics of the Latin culture. Millions of children in Latin America never go to school, and the majority of those who do rarely get beyond the third or fourth grade. On the other hand, the ideal of an education for each child is so strongly imbedded in our culture, is so closely associated with principles of equality, and is so deeply cherished by middle-class families—the group from which most missionaries are drawn—that it has virtually become an integral part of Christianity itself.

Moreover, primary education has been a fertile field for the missionary to cultivate. This is the second reason why primary schools have been emphasized by religious agencies. A sizable proportion of Latin-American families want their children to have some education. The desire may not always be strong, and commonly accepted standards of adequacy may be low, but a goodly proportion of families would like their children to be able to read, write, and "do common figgering." For at least twenty-five years and in some countries for a longer period, there have been small but growing groups of intellectuals working for widespread education of the common people. Missionaries have found their desire to educate the children of the masses both acceptable to many families and compatible with an important new intellectual movement.

Finally, missionaries have emphasized primary schools because they adhere to the belief, widespread among denominations, that the best and most efficient means of spreading the principles of Christianity is to start with the children. That the molding of a true Christian character can be done most easily by beginning in the formative years of a child's life is common doctrine among all faiths and most denominations.

The missionary found in the lack of elementary education, so normal in most Latin-American countries, a problem which provided an excellent outlet for his religious motivation and which challenged his sense of democracy. In characteristic North American fashion he tackled the problem by a simple and direct approach. He organized, financed, and supervised schools—large numbers of schools that taught reading, writing, and arithmetic to thousands of children, many of whom would not otherwise have set foot in a schoolroom.

Numerous primary schools incorporate only the first three or four grades, particularly those not directly associated with secondary schools. It is conventional practice for a school to offer work only in the first grade at the time of organization and to add a grade each year thereafter if there are sufficient funds, teachers, and students. There are missionary schools that began this way and now offer courses from kindergarten through high school, but they are extraordinary. Most of the primary schools find it difficult to expand beyond the third or fourth grade. Limited funds, a student body expected to go to work at an early age, and an isolated location which discourages qualified teachers handicap the schools. Some denominations appear to put their resources into numerous small schools instead of enlarging a few.

Sometimes, because the missionaries busy themselves with hiring teachers, paying salaries, obtaining supplies, and keeping accounts, rural pupils rarely see the men whose schools they attend. In other instances the missionary teaches one or two classes. In nearly all cases the familiar teachers are natives of the country in which the school is located. Where the primary school is part of a large institution, offering both primary and secondary training, the influence of the missionaries is usually strongest.

Even in those situations, however, it is rare that the primary school is a replica of the common elementary school in the United States. It is not only that the physical facilities are usually more meager, with a minimum of teaching equipment and materials; but instructional methods are quite different, the relationship between teacher and student is more stilted and formal, and less recognition is given to the different abilities and interests of the developing child as he moves from one age level to another.

The common method of instruction is for the teacher to dictate the lesson or write it on the blackboard and for the student to copy it in his notebook and commit it to memory. This process of dictating, copying, and memorizing for examinations goes on day after day, with little opportunity for the student to develop his creative talents or to learn the crucial characteristics of his home and community environment. The elements of problem-solving, other than by the rules of arithmetic, are certainly not emphasized by the common methods of teaching. Moreover, the content of courses is circumscribed by rules and regulations issued by the ministries of education. Students are commonly promoted from one grade to the next on the basis of examinations administered by bureaucratic representatives. This means that the students of a teacher who strays very far from the prescribed subject matter will not do well at examination time, and the teacher runs the risk of jeopardizing his own standing with both parents and colleagues.

Nearly all Protestant missionaries engaged in primary or secondary educational work point to close governmental supervision of curriculums and to the dictation method of teaching as frustrating impediments to their activities. This complaint is not so common among Catholic missionaries because many parochial schools in the United States stress memory work. Some Catholics, however, are none too pleased with the strict governmental control of curriculums.

Although primary schools are by all odds the most numerous technical projects sponsored by religious agencies in Latin America, the secondary schools are not without significance. They are a great deal more influential than their number implies. In most Latin-American countries the standard primary school covers the first four to six years of training, from which those who finish can go on to another five or six years of instruction in a secondary school. Thus the latter is, from some points of view, a combination of what we usually call "junior high" and "senior high" in the United States. Graduates of the secondary schools receive a Bachelor's degree which carries somewhat more prestige than a high-school diploma in North America, and in some fields of study the curriculum is probably more advanced than in the ordinary high school in the United States.

The graduates of the secondary schools usually enter the university for further study, become teachers in primary schools, or take white-collar jobs. Those who continue their studies through the university often become government employees, and many of them occupy posts of considerable power and prestige.

Graduates of the secondary schools sponsored by religious agencies help perpetuate the whole missionary movement, especially the Protestant element of it. Usually, few students in the secondary schools are of the Protestant faith, but these schools are training grounds from which come many of the teachers in the Protestant primary schools, pastors for Protestant churches, secretaries and assistants to missionaries, and businessmen who are sympathetic and helpful to the work of the missionaries. Graduates of these schools, regardless of their religious affiliations, are likely to carry through life a respect for their alma mater.

Like the primary schools, the secondary schools follow the curriculum prescribed by the ministry of education of the country in which they are located. Most of the teachers are natives of the country and are university or normal-school graduates. The staff sent by the sponsoring religious agency usually includes the director of the school, perhaps an assistant director, teachers of English, and sometimes one or two teachers of specialized subjects added to the curriculum over and above the requirements of the ministry of education. Secondary-school students are normally upper-middle-class young people.

Many secondary schools, particularly those that have a primary school under the same management at the same site, are virtually self-supporting institutions. The contributions which they receive from their sponsoring agency are small in relation to the amounts which they receive from tuition and, in some countries, from grants made by the government. Some of them have received large, lump-sum donations from individuals for the construction of their principal buildings—donations from both North America and Latin America.

A few of the larger secondary schools are relatively free to follow the teaching methods and examination practices which they choose, but even these, since they depend primarily on native teachers, must employ the traditional teaching methods. However, the influence of the sponsors is usually seen in the selection of well-prepared teachers, who take their jobs seriously and who conduct themselves capably in the classroom and in the community; the encouragement of self-discipline among the students; an attitude of partnership between teacher and pupil, who respect each other; the introduction of extracurricular activities, particularly group games and sports; and concentrated study of English. Because of emphasis along these lines, many schools have won a position of respect in the countries in which they operate. Some of them have long waiting lists of applicants and turn away many students who would like to enter.

Several of them have been in operation for more than a quarter of a century. Although it can hardly be said that they have brought about fundamental changes in the Latin-American system of secondary education, the better ones stand as excellent examples for those who want to modernize the system. Many of these schools have turned out graduates who occupy important posts, both public and private, within their respective countries—men and women who received a better education than would probably have been the case, had they not attended one of these schools.

Most of the fifty-eight technical schools represented in Table 5 are little more than vocational and commercial departments of large secondary schools. Some are separate institutions in which the central core of study is clearly technical in nature. Others are semi-independent schools, though nominally subordinate to larger institutions, with a specialized curriculum and with their own standards of admission and requirements for graduation. Information is not available by which to make a clear-cut separation between the three types. Altogether, it is quite evident that religious agencies have not made a heavy impact on the area of vocational, commercial, and industrial training.

Many, if not most, of the large secondary schools operate commercial departments, in which students are taught typing, shorthand, bookkeeping, and commercial law. These are integrated as a field of specialization for students during the last two or three years of their secondary-school work, much like commercial departments in North American high schools. Those who take these courses are sought by business firms; many of them, because of their superior training in English, are particularly valuable to importing or exporting firms or to the subsidiaries of North American companies.

A few of the secondary schools also have departments or some interrelated courses in home economics. These are, however, small in number compared to commercial departments. Where they do exist, they attract few students, for it is rare that a girl whose parents can afford to send her to one of the secondary schools is interested in home economics. Most of them will have servants in their homes to take care of the cooking, sewing, and children. Moreover, there are relatively few jobs available for girls who specialize in home economics, though they are increasing slowly. One or two missionary schools have the distinction of first offering home economics courses in the countries in which they are located. The status of women in Latin-American society will perhaps have to be raised considerably before home economics becomes a profession of importance.

Specialized agricultural schools, on the other hand, are more numerous than those in home economics, attract more students, and appear to be influencing the culture slightly but steadily. Most of those that are under the auspices of religious agencies are serving young people below the university level. They usually draw their students from among farm boys who have had four to six years of primary schooling, and the boys, most of whom are boarding students, spend three or four hours each day working on the mission farm. The course of study, lasting three or four years, customarily includes training in Spanish, mathematics, geography, and some work in the social sciences, in addition to the specialized agricultural courses. Nevertheless, the graduates of these schools are sometimes so poorly prepared in fundamentals that they have a difficult time finding positions in which they can capitalize on their agricultural knowledge. In most of the Latin-American countries the graduates of these schools are not admitted to universities because they have not had the necessary preparation in a recognized secondary school. It is probable, if this type of agricultural school is to make a really pervasive contribution to Latin-American agriculture, that it will have to change its curriculum so as to turn out students with a better foundation in non-agricultural subjects.

There are a few schools sponsored by the religious agencies which give specialized training in carpentry, masonry, mechanics, machine-shop, and electrical work. Such training, usually for primary-school boys, often takes the form of practical courses added to the regular curriculum. On the whole, such shopwork does not represent an important aspect of the technical service work of the agencies. Apparently, persons skilled in mechanical craftsmanship rarely turn to missionary work.

Health Activities

Health projects are the second principal interest of the religious agencies in Latin America. There are at least 119 hospitals and clinics sponsored by such agencies in 19 of the Latin-American countries. Annexed to several of the hospitals are nurses' training schools. The distribution of the hospitals and clinics is given in Table 6.[2] The only Latin-American countries in which the United States religious agencies do not seem to have clinics or hospitals are Panama and Uruguay.

Many of the medical institutions are small treatment-rooms or

2. Arranged from information in Department of State Publication No. 4422, as supplemented by field work and data from the Missionary Research Library and the Mission Secretariat.

clinics located at rural mission posts or in working-class areas of urban centers. Others are large, modern, well-equipped hospitals. The independent clinics are often staffed with one or two American-trained nurses, who work under the general supervision of a local doctor. In some rural posts a missionary who has had no medical training may give inoculations and dispense simple medicines. In urban centers the larger clinics and hospitals regularly have from one to three North American doctors, several North American nurses, all of whom are medical missionaries, and a sizable staff of local doctors, midwives, and nurses. Most of these institutions are from 60 to 80 per cent self-supporting from fees and the sale of medicines.

TABLE 6

Argentina	2	Guatemala	6
Bolivia	9	Haiti	4
Brazil	16	Honduras	4
Chile	11	Mexico	19
Colombia	9	Nicaragua	10
Costa Rica	1	Paraguay	4
Cuba	5	Peru	4
Dominican Republic	1	Venezuela	3
Ecuador	4	British possessions	6
El Salvador	1		

The missionaries appear to be bringing medical care to relatively large numbers of people who need it and who probably would not otherwise receive it. Doctors, nurses, clinics, and hospitals are in short supply in Latin America. Diseases and parasites are widespread. The average life-expectancy is short where thousands of rural people never have the services of the medical profession. The medical missionaries are helping to close the gap between the need for medical services and the availability of such services, but rarely are they introducing new techniques or methods not already known by many local doctors.

There is an enormous need in most Latin-American countries for greatly increased emphasis on programs of environmental sanitation; for teaching the ordinary family a few simple practices of personal hygiene; and for inculcating habits of living, eating, and drinking which prevent disease and lessen the ravages of parasites. However, there is a remarkably small amount of this type of work being done by missionaries. They have a tendency to stick to their institutions, treating only people who are already sick. Many inoculations against epidemic diseases are given at the clinics and hospitals, which, of course, is an important form of preventive medicine. Moreover, many of the doctors in rural areas travel to villages near their established posts for regularly scheduled clinics. In these instances, however, their work is usually to treat the sick. They rarely practice preventive medicine, at least in the form of educational or community-organization programs aimed at getting the people to create a more healthful environment. A change of emphasis from treating those who are already sick to preventing people from falling sick appears to be possible and to offer an opportunity for much wider service to increased numbers of people.

Agricultural Activities

In addition to the agricultural schools discussed previously, the agricultural projects of the United States religious agencies are of two main types, namely, farms and programs of extension education. In many instances both types of project are connected with a school, and it is rare to find an extension program which does not emanate from a mission post on a farm. The number of agricultural projects, by countries, is shown in Table 7.[3]

TABLE 7

Argentina	1	Honduras	2
Bolivia	7	Mexico	4
Brazil	5	Nicaragua	1
Chile	3	Peru	2
Colombia	2	Venezuela	2
Costa Rica	1	British possessions	2
Educador	7		—
Guatemala	4	Total	43

The majority of these projects are farms, and most of the farms are used primarily to produce food for the missionaries and their students. It is not uncommon for lunches to be served to the pupils of a primary school on a farm, and boarding-schools often coexist with the farms. In the latter case, of course, there is a considerable demand for locally produced food.

3. Arranged from information in the sources used for Table 6.

Even though the products of the farms move principally to the mission kitchen, the missionaries frequently introduce new crops or try out new practices that appear to have promise for the community in general. Moreover, many of the farms lend purebred studs —bulls, rams, and boars—to neighboring farmers. On the demonstration plots of mission farms, there is often some experimental work with crop varieties and fertilizing practices.

Most of the farms visited during the field survey were operating at a financial loss. In no instance was this because primary emphasis was placed on experimental or demonstration work. Agricultural experiment stations are not ordinarily expected to make a profit, but on some of the mission farms there is no experimental work at all, and in most cases it represents a minor part of the total operation. A surprisingly large proportion of the farms are situated on extremely poor land. In a few cases this has been a deliberate policy of the sponsoring agency, for it wants to show what can be done in the way of rehabilitating worn-out soil. In other cases it has probably resulted from an unwillingness or inability of the agency to pay the price necessary to get good land. Poor soil is unquestionably one explanation of why many of the farms do not pay expenses. Some of them are in such isolated places that there is no opportunity to send their products to market. In a few cases the managers know little about farming, particularly in tropical areas.

Although most of the farms lose money, there are a few which are outstanding financial successes. Some of them not only pay their operating expenses and interest on the investment but also produce a surplus, which is used to support schools and similar activities of the missionaries. Even among the best of them, however, there is not much indication that they have made significant contributions to improving agriculture in the surrounding areas. Some of them have livestock, farming practices, and experimental results that are well worth the attention of their neighbors. These really good farms rarely are managed by persons interested in sharing their findings and accomplishments with surrounding farmers. In some instances well-planned activities would push the influence of the mission farms far beyond their boundaries.

The agricultural extension education projects vary widely in scope and effectiveness. Most of them are in the nature of personal services rendered to neighboring farmers by the agriculturist—donating small supplies of seeds or planting-stock of a new crop; assisting in vaccinating livestock; selling insecticides at cost and explaining their use; or simply discussing farm problems during neighborly visits, with occasional suggestions about something new that might wisely be attempted by the farmer. In some of the extension projects there is a program for aiding farmers to organize study groups or to encourage the growth of purchasing and marketing co-operatives. Projects of this type, however, in which the missionary approaches the problem of extension education through group activities and encourages farmers to tackle their problems through their own collective efforts, are rare. This is partly because the missionaries usually focus their attention on assisting low-income, socially depressed farmers—people who lack the education, experience, and psychological stamina to "stand on their own feet" and assume the responsibilities for improving their community situation, as distinguished from changing their individual farming practices. It is also partly because a paternalistic type of extension work, with emphasis on rendering direct services to farmers, is easy compared with the task of helping people to help themselves.

There are, without question, real opportunities for improving extension-type projects and starting new ones. The chief difficulty appears to be the lack of knowledge on the part of many agricultural missionaries about how to do really effective extension work. The agriculturist is often so busy carrying on the farming operations that he does not have time to develop an extension program. Furthermore, there seems to be a psychological hesitancy on the part of many of the agricultural missionaries to "break away" from their farms in order to get out into the surrounding communities. The general churchworkers and evangelists have little timidity in going out to preach, but the agriculturist appears to have less confidence in his ideas about improving farming than the evangelist does in his ideas about saving souls.

4 SELECTED CASE STUDIES

The nature of the religious agencies' technical work can be described in general terms, as in the preceding chapters, but it can also be represented by examples. Farm, school, and clinic are brought closer to the reader when their successes are made tangible in the following case studies. Varied as the missions are varied, these studies collectively constitute a fair sample.

Educational Institutions

From what has been said in earlier chapters, three points should *quote* be evident about the prevailing system of education in most Latin-American countries. The policies, curriculums, and teaching methods of most educational institutions are dominated by upper-class values and ideas. Emphasis on classical subjects crowds out the teaching of applied science and vocational skills. Most children get no schooling beyond the third or fourth grade.

From almost any point of view the educational situation in Latin *quote* America is not good. Too few children go to school, and too few of those who do go are equipped with the kinds of knowledge and skill that enable them to make the greatest contribution to the progress of their countries. Religious agencies from the United States cannot reasonably be expected to contribute much toward providing educational opportunities for the millions of children who at the present time are getting almost no formal training. The task is much too big for any group of private agencies to handle. Their work could, however, be important as a series of pilot demonstrations of desirable educational programs, and the graduates of their schools could become the leaders and teachers of improved educational methods and standards.

The following three cases are examples of mission schools that are operated by traditional methods. They are at peace with their environment and, by some standards, are achieving tangible and valuable results.

41

INSTITUTO AMERICANO (COCHABAMBA, BOLIVIA)

The American Institute, situated in the outskirts of Cochabamba, is a combined primary and secondary school for both boys and girls. It is operated by North American Methodist missionaries supported by their church in the United States. The institute was started in Cochabamba in 1912 and moved to its present location, a 6–8-acre tract of rough land, in 1949. It has two large buildings and living facilities for the North American staff, which, in 1953, consisted of three married couples and one unmarried man. It has classes from the kindergarten through the twelfth grade.

Most of the students live in the city and are transported to and from the school in special busses. A few students—usually about 30—live in a dormitory section of one of the school buildings. Most of the latter are children of plantation-owners, whose homes lie outside the city. The great majority of students are from families in the middle- and upper-income groups. Not more than 20 per cent are from homes of working-class families. Tuition ranged from 1,000 to 1,500 bolivianos per month, in 1953, which in terms of then prevailing exchange rates equaled less than $5.00. Nevertheless, the ordinary Bolivian workman would have to make very great sacrifices to send his children to the American Institute.

In most outward appearances this school is similar to those found in thousands of small cities in the United States. The buildings are reasonably adequate for the 750–800 students. The school term is ten months each year. The staff is primarily Bolivian, but each of the seven staff members from the United States teaches one or more classes.

The director and assistant director, both relatively young men, usually perform pastoral duties in addition to their teaching and administrative responsibilities at the institute. Until midsummer of 1953, the director of the school was pastor of the local English-speaking Methodist congregation and the assistant director was pastor of the local Spanish-speaking Methodist church. These duties, however, were not great time-consumers. The congregations are small, and the number of church activities few. At the school, there is one hour of required religious instruction each week and a regular chapel service. The former is given by Protestants, mainly the North American staff members, but most of the students and several of the Bolivian teachers are Catholic. The majority of parents send their children to the school because they think it is a good one, not because of its Methodist or Protestant connections.

The institute conforms to all the legal and regulatory requirements governing primary and secondary schools in Bolivia. Its curriculum, like that of other Bolivian schools, is set forth in considerable detail by ministry of education regulations. There is practically no leeway as to what courses will be given or in what year they will be offered. Moreover, there is fairly strict control as to the material that must be covered in each subject and the progress that each student must make in order to pass from one grade to another. Not only are there periodic inspections by officials, who enforce these regulations, but at the end of each year special examiners appointed by the ministry sit with each of the teachers to determine which of the children shall pass to the next higher grade. This system, regardless of its

TABLE 8

Subject	Hours per Week	Subject	Hours per Week
Algebra.............	2	Chemistry...........	3
Biology.............	2	Literature...........	4
Physics.............	3	Psychology..........	4
English.............	2	Geography..........	2
History.............	2	Religion.............	1
Civics.............	1	Music.............	2
Art................	1		—
Physical education....	2	Total..........	33
Geometry...........	2		

merits, permits very few innovations. Neither the staff nor the sponsoring agency can show much creativeness or import many new ideas, as long as the school conforms to the established pattern of courses.

In the last three years of high school, students can elect to take a commercial course, which prepares them for secretarial and bookkeeping jobs. Other than this, no vocational subjects are offered. Many of the graduates of the institute become teachers in primary schools, but there are no courses in educational methods or teacher-training in the curriculum.

In some countries, schools of this type are able to add one or two courses to the required curriculum and thus train their students a little more broadly than the law requires. In Bolivia this is virtually impossible because of the heavy load of work that would be imposed on the student. For example, the courses required in the noncommercial curriculum for high-school students in the tenth grade are listed in Table 8. There is not a single year in high school in which the student takes less than twelve subjects.

In addition to the curricular strait jacket, the teaching methods are traditionally one-sided. Most of the Bolivian teachers instruct by dictation. They either write the lessons on the blackboard or present them orally in such a clear, precise, slow manner that the students can copy in their notebooks much of what is said. There is little classroom discussion; the whole emphasis is on memory work. Teachers are careful to present material in a succinct, orderly manner so that it can be easily committed to memory by the student. Rarely are students taught the relation between what they are studying in their textbooks and the environment in which they live. There is much emphasis on learning a long list of characteristics of some particular object or process being studied, but little practice in understanding the crucial and fundamental interrelations among these characteristics. Even in mathematics, there is a minimum of problem-solving and a maximum of memorizing the operational rules, theorems, and corollaries.

Within the existing tradition-bound framework of educational ideas and practices, the American Institute in Cochabamba is a good school. The teachers are well qualified, energetic, and stay on the job. The students are provided with reasonably adequate facilities, in a wholesome Christian atmosphere, in which to study and learn. There is no attempt to force Methodism or any other creed on unsuspecting youngsters. The school is turning out graduates—about 800 of them since its inception—who go on to universities for further study, take positions as secretaries or bookkeepers, become primary-school teachers, or go into the family business. In general, they are probably better qualified than most of the graduates of other available schools. They are likely, for instance, to be more proficient in English. They are reputedly honest, forthright, well-integrated people who will always remember with respect and pleasure their association with the North American staff at the school.

COLEGIO DEL TEPEYAC (MEXICO CITY, MEXICO)

Colegio del Tepeyac is a primary, secondary, and preparatory school for boys, situated in an upper-class, residential area and operated by Benedictine priests from St. John's Abbey, Collegeville, Minnesota. A private lay school until late in 1946, the Colegio has been under its present sponsorship only since 1947. During their first five years the Benedictines operated a primary and a secondary school, which, in accordance with Mexican standards, provided six years of work in the primary grades and three years at the secondary level. In 1952 an additional two years of preparatory or junior-college work was added to the curriculum.

The school has grown from about 500 students in 1947 to an enrolment of approximately 1,700 in 1954. About 1,150 boys are in the primary grades, 450 in the secondary, and approximately 100 at the preparatory level. The total capacity of the excellent buildings is about 1,900. The students are mainly from middle- and upper-income families living in the surrounding suburbs. There are no boarding students. Most of the teachers are Mexicans, but all of the Benedictines teach some courses, mainly ethics, logic, English, Latin, and Greek. They also function as assistants in some of the neighboring parishes, although most of their time is given to the school.

TABLE 9

APPROVED SUBJECTS

Subject	Years Studied	Subject	Years Studied
Mathematics.........	3	History.............	3
Biology.............	3	Spanish.............	3
Geography..........	3	English.............	3
Chemistry..........	1	Civics..............	3
Physics............	1	Music..............	3
Drawing............	2	Physical training.....	3
Manual training......	3		

The Colegio is fully accredited at primary, secondary, and preparatory levels by the secretary of education. It therefore follows the required curriculum, summarized in Table 9, for the three years of secondary work. Classes in each of the subjects meet for fifty-minute periods from two to five times per week.

This curriculum is generally similar to that for high-school students in other Latin-American countries, but three years of manual training are required. This indicates that Mexican educational authorities have recognized that vocational courses, in which the student learns to work with his hands, are proper subjects for study in high school. It may be an important indicator of the extent to which Mexico has broken with past traditions and is accepting many ideas and value-judgments now prevalent in the United States. Also, no doubt, it stems in part from the industrialization which has occurred in Mexico more than in most Latin-American countries and the consequent demand for skilled workers. The manual training courses taught at Colegio del Tepeyac are bookbinding, leather-work, and electromechanics.

The presence of these courses in this particular school is significant as a clue to recent Mexican educational theory, but it is not direct evidence of the nature of the Colegio. The priests in charge are little interested in manual training, and their students come from families socially above such work. If one of these students cannot carry the heavy schedule of languages, mathematics, and sciences, he is likely to leave the Colegio for a clerical job or a course in a business school.

At the preparatory level, which follows the six years of primary and the three years of secondary study, there are four fields of specialization—law, accounting, engineering, and architecture. The two years of preparatory work are pointed specifically toward fitting the student to enter a university, and he is called on to choose his general field of specialization when he has finished nine years of primary and secondary study. This is similar to requiring high-school Sophomores in the United States to decide on the course of study which they would take in a university and to spend the last two years of high school preparing specifically for their university course.

The level of work required in the two years of preparatory study can be shown by the record of a student who studied engineering. This student took more mathematics after two years of algebra and one year of a combined course in plane geometry and trigonometry during his secondary course. The two years of mathematics at the preparatory level included one semester each of trigonometry, advanced algebra, analytic geometry, and calculus. In addition, he took chemistry and physics in each of the two years and one year each of physical geography, cosmography, hygiene, history of Mexico, etymology, mechanical drawing, philosophy, world literature, logic, and ethics.

The curriculum in both the secondary and preparatory courses is obviously a difficult one for many students. It entails much homework and permits few extracurricular activities besides team sports and intramural games.

In practically all respects, Colegio del Tepeyac "measures up" to parochial schools in the United States. Six of its graduates are now studying in the United States to become priests, and one is studying in Rome after a three-year American course. The plan is for these boys to return to Mexico and become priests after they have served for a few years as faculty members of the Colegio. One of the important functions of the school is to train young men for the priesthood.

The tuition charges in 1954 were 55 pesos per month in primary, 65 in secondary, and 75 in preparatory. This was roughly equivalent to $6.50, $7.60, and $8.80. These fees, high compared to those of other religious agencies in Mexico City, enable Colegio del Tepeyac to build a reserve and to repay the original investment of approximately $300,000 made by the mother abbey. The tuition is well beyond the reach of working-class families.

Mexican anticlerical law not only prohibits the teaching of religion in schools but also prevents churches from owning school buildings and facilities. It has partially obstructed some educational activities of United States religious agencies in Mexico. In most instances, however, these agencies have complied without suffering. In the case of Colegio del Tepeyac the school property is owned by a corporation of five Mexican citizens. The corporation rents the property, at a nominal charge, to a lay teacher who operates it as a private school. The Benedictine priests who manage and direct it are theoretically acting for this lay teacher.[1]

COLEGIO INTERNACIONAL (ASUNCIÓN, PARAGUAY)

International College is a primary and secondary school for both boys and girls. It is sponsored by the denomination known as the "Disciples of Christ." As in other schools of this type in Paraguay, there are six years of primary and six years of secondary work. Graduates of the school are qualified to enter a university. The school was started in 1920 as a small, first-grade school for boys. It followed the common procedure of adding a grade each year, until it received a substantial grant from a family in Ohio in 1926, which enabled it to construct new buildings and become a large, coeducational institution meeting the requirements of the ministry of education for primary and secondary schools in Paraguay. It now has an excellent physical plant in one of the rich residential sections of Asunción.

In recent years the school has enrolled over 600 students, most of whom

1. A practice more commonly followed, especially among Protestant agencies, is for the classroom property to be transferred to the government, while the near-by dormitories and living facilities are retained as the property of the religious agency. The teachers in the school are employees of the department of education. The Protestant missionaries restrict their activities to operating the dormitories, in which, of course, they can give religious instruction. This means, however, that their influence is usually quite limited in case of non-boarding students.

came from middle- and upper-class families. There are usually 20–25 boarding students—all girls. Members of the American colony in Asunción send their children to this school, but the percentage of North American students is quite low. All subjects are taught in Spanish, but English as a subject is offered from the first year of primary school through the twelfth grade. A majority of students come from Catholic homes; but, notwithstanding, any student may attend. Two classes per week introduce religious instruction—mainly Bible stories—to primary students; otherwise, there is slight emphasis on religious instruction. Most of the teachers are Paraguayan. The teachers from the United States, of whom there were six in 1953, in addition to the director and his wife, hold English and Bible

TABLE 10

APPROVED SUBJECTS

Subject	Years Studied	Subject	Years Studied
Spanish	6	Mineralogy and geology	1
Latin	5	Psychology	1
English	6	Anatomy and physiol-	
Mathematics	4	ogy	1
Geography	4	Philosophy	3
Biology	3	Art and penmanship	3
Chemistry	2	Civics and economics	2
Physics	1	Hygiene	1

classes. One of them also teaches a one-year course in home economics, which has been added to the required secondary curriculum.

Students in the primary grades attend classes for five and one-half hours per day for five days each week; those at the secondary level spend a six-day week of five hours per day in school. Many of the graduates go to a university for further study, and many of those who do not meet the requirements for a diploma continue their studies in business schools. Table 10 lists the subjects required in the six years of high school. From two to five hours of instruction per week in each subject means a total of thirty hours of required classwork. The religious instruction and home economics course—not shown in the table—have been added to the required curriculum.

This kind of classical Latin-American course seldom correlates life in the home and community and life in the school. The student steps out of his regular environment while he attends classes. The dictation method of teaching is common but apparently not followed to the extreme that it is in most Paraguayan schools. Even so, the curriculum and the methods of instruction are based on the theory that there is a given body of worthwhile knowledge to be passed on from generation to generation and that the most efficient way to do this is to have schools in which teachers organize this knowledge into convenient packages for students to commit to memory.

International College receives about $1,000 per year from its sponsoring agency in the United States, plus a few miscellaneous gifts and $9,600 per year in salaries for the eight North American missionaries on its directing and teaching staff. Except for these funds, the school is operated from tuition fees. These range from 100 guarani per month in kindergarten to 190 in secondary. This was roughly equivalent in 1953 to $2.00–$4.00 per month, a sum well beyond the range of working-class families in Paraguay.

These three schools—Instituto Americano, Colegio del Tepeyac, and Colegio Internacional—are fairly typical of a large number of primary and secondary schools operated by the agencies. Within the prevailing framework of required curriculums and customary teaching practices, they are good schools. Indeed, they are probably better than the majority of public schools of their same general type. They are urban schools serving upper-class families, and among such families they have a good reputation. Children who attend them are often envied by their friends and neighbors. Many of their graduates, after attending a university, become influential citizens. Schools of this type no doubt stimulate neighboring educational institutions by the examples they set in trained teachers, thorough methods, and wholesome physical environments.

In one sense, however, they are failing to cope with some of the fundamental problems of Latin America. Both Bolivia and Paraguay are desperately poor countries. Over half the people of the former are Indians, who cling to old traditions and customs, many of whom live at the lowest imaginable level of existence. The situation in Mexico is better than it is in Paraguay and Bolivia, but still Mexico contains thousands of subsistence farmers who produce most of the things they eat and wear and who live outside a regular commercial economy.

Latin America needs citizens scientifically trained to be good farmers; it needs mechanics, electricians, and carpenters who are adept at their trades; masons, plumbers, and plasterers who are able and efficient workmen; and numerous other skilled artisans. Bolivia has lived for many years on the exportation of one or two mineral products, has done little to improve agriculture or develop industry, and imports large quantities of food, even though there are great areas of rich, undeveloped land. Paraguay, with no mineral exports and with large tracts of unused land, has made extremely little progress in improving and modernizing its old patterns and methods of farming. Mexico has moved forward in industry and scientific agriculture, but there are still segments of the Mexican economy in which productivity per worker is very low.

Schools alone cannot solve these problems of undeveloped resources side by side with underemployed, unskilled people, but there is no denying the need for graduates who can make a start. It is by applying technology to everyday problems, by developing a skilled and imaginative labor force, and by solving managerial problems that the United States has contributed most to modern civilization. These are the patterns that North Americans can most readily help other countries to imitate. Yet, as in the three schools just reviewed, many religious agencies are bringing little to Latin America in the way of needed educational innovations of the sort which North Americans have inherited and practiced.

The problem posed by this anomaly, though a tragic and serious one, is by no means easy to solve. As shown by later ca[se studies], significant progress has been made by some agencies u[nder some] conditions, but the door to social change is not readily [and easily] opened. Traditional school patterns are buttressed by a c[omplicated] set of static social and cultural values. In countries like B[olivia and] Paraguay and until recently in Mexico, the people who [made the] laws and sanctioned the customs pertaining to education [belonged] to a small group of upper-class families. Many of their ch[ildren cus]tomarily went to Europe or the United States to study, a[nd a large] proportion of them became lawyers, doctors, diplomats, [and gov]ernment officials. These families wanted a primary- and s[econdary-] school system which would ground their children in thes[e fields of] endeavor. They did not want their boys to become mech[anics and] carpenters or their girls to become secretaries and home economists. Consequently, they were not willing to support institutions, through either tuition fees or taxes, which turned out skilled artisans and agriculturists.

What, for instance, would be the likely results if the American Institute in Cochabamba wanted to bring its curriculum into line with the needs of the country? At the present time the Methodist church, through its foreign mission board, pays the salaries of the United States personnel, amounting to about $8,000 per year, and gives about $1,500 per year for operating expenses; the institute is self-supporting otherwise. If its curriculum were altered by substitution of vocational courses for some of those now required—a type of change in line with Bolivia's needs—not only would the school have to obtain governmental permission, but its investment in plant and equipment would rise, and teaching costs would probably go up because of the smaller classes usually necessary in vocational education. Moreover, its graduates would no longer be able to enter the universities or normal schools for further study. Students who transferred from the institute to other primary or secondary schools would probably lose credits. Upper-income families would have little interest in sending their children to a technical school, and receipts from tuition would be reduced. The institute would go bankrupt unless it were subsidized by the sponsoring agency.

This kind of problem hinders school directors in Latin America. Perhaps they might start small technical schools for students who had finished the primary grades, as increments to their present systems, subsidizing them with earnings from the primary schools or from greater donations by sponsoring agencies. There are countries in Latin America—and Bolivia may be one of them—where new ideas and revised government policies are coming into prominence and power so rapidly that mission teachers may find themselves in the camps of the conservatives and reactionaries instead of leading, unless they make changes of this character.

Fortunately, some schools sponsored by religious agencies are not so tightly bound by old customs and traditions. The four following case histories of institutions that are making new contributions to the basic needs of Latin America amplify this.

INSTITUTO MACKENZIE (SÃO PAULO, BRAZIL)

Mackenzie Institute is one of the outstanding schools in South America. It started as a small Presbyterian mission school over eighty years ago and has grown into one of the prime educational institutions in Brazil. It is located in the heart of one of the fastest-growing industrial centers in the world. It has shared in São Paulo's rapid growth, has contributed to its industrialization, has made itself respected in the community, and has pioneered new and significant educational practices in Brazil. It is far from being typical of educational institutions sponsored by religious agencies, but it is a noteworthy example of how one agency has made its influence felt over wide and important areas of Brazilian life.

In 1953, Mackenzie Institute, which had a total enrolment of about 5,000 students, consisted of the following schools:

1. A primary school, which offered work from kindergarten through a fifth year. In accord with regular educational practice in Brazil, the last year of the primary school was a special preparatory course for junior high school.

2. A junior high school with four years of work. This type of school is called *Ginasio* in Brazil.

3. A senior high school, which offered two curriculums, both for three years of study. One, a general classical curriculum, prepared students for either a normal school or a college of arts and sciences in a university. The other, the "classical-scientific" curriculum, prepared students for studying engineering, architecture, or science in a university.

4. A commercial school open to students who have finished junior high. One of its curriculums provided three years of training in secretarial work; the other, a three-year course in accounting. This commercial school is similar to many of the specialized vocational high schools in the United States. Each curriculum required three years of Portuguese, three years of science, two years of mathematics, and two or three years of English. The secretarial curriculum required three years of English and two of French. There was also a two-year correspondence course which led to a diploma but not to a recognized certificate of graduation.

5. A technical school, which was open to students who had finished junior high or an accepted vocational trade school and who had passed a special entrance examination. This school had three curriculums. One was a four-year course in industrial chemistry, the second a three-year

course in electromechanics, and the third a three-year course in land surveying. This was a practical school with requirements below the university level of work.

6. A university, with faculties of engineering, architecture, arts and science, business administration, and law. The requirements for the degree usually necessitate five years of full-time study in engineering, architecture, and law; three years in arts and science; and four years in business administration. (The law faculty is newly organized, having offered its first courses in 1954–55.)

There are at least three significant points to be noted from this list of schools: first, Mackenzie offers educational opportunities from the very first year of study through a university; second, the commercial and technical schools offer practical or vocational training for those students who are not interested in, or do not have the ability for, pursuing the regular high-school course; third, and most important, the emphasis placed on commercial and industrial subjects indicates that Mackenzie has been responsive to the needs of the rapidly expanding commerce and industry of São Paulo. In fact, it has been more than responsive to the needs of its environment; it has helped create that environment. By turning out secretaries, accountants, skilled artisans, engineers, architects, and junior business executives, it has contributed to the development of one of the great commercial and industrial centers of Latin America. This is an important reason why it is an integral and respected part of its community.

Mackenzie has introduced new and venturesome ideas and practices and has adapted them to existing conditions in ways that have been acceptable. For instance, when the very first primary school was started in 1870, boys and girls were seated together in the same classes—a practice not yet common in Latin-American countries. Instruction has always been available to students of all faiths, denominations, and races. Mackenzie organized the first technical school at a level lower than university training, a type of school now common in Brazil but still rare in most Latin-American countries. Mackenzie introduced basketball to Brazil, and the first soccer game played in Brazil matched Mackenzie students against a German club about fifty years ago. Today, soccer is the national game in Brazil, a sport as widespread as baseball in the United States. The department of physical education has long been important at Mackenzie, and many teachers from surrounding areas come to study its organization and methods. As early as 1900, two or three of Mackenzie's teachers were hired to help reorganize the public school system of São Paulo. Mackenzie's library was started by a Brazilian girl who had been sent to the United States to study library science and who now directs the public library in São Paulo.

All Mackenzie's schools conform to government requirements and are subject to government inspection, but this has not always been true. It is possible that some of the school's successes resulted from the freedom that it enjoyed in past years. For instance, from the time of its founding in 1896 until 1927, when it was given its autonomy, the school of engineering functioned under the direction of New York University. In 1932 it lost its own curriculum, which was patterned after that of colleges in the United States, and was forced to conform to the standard Brazilian curriculum. Nevertheless, it has maintained a camp in the country, to give its engineering students field experience; field work is required for the engineering degree. No other university in Brazil has such a camp for engineering students. Moreover, in all the schools, teachers pass or fail their own students on the basis of examinations which they design, and there is relatively little of the dictation method of teaching. Most of these teachers are Brazilians.

Mackenzie, named for a New Yorker who donated $50,000 about 1896, has been self-supporting since it purchased the land on which its present buildings are located. However, its acquisition of a plant now worth several million dollars was due in part to the Presbyterian Mission Board, which loaned it $25,000 in 1932, later declaring $10,000 of the sum as a gift. The primary and secondary schools make money that is used to support the university, and a large part of the budget has been furnished since 1954 by an annual federal grant of 5,000,000 cruzeiros, equivalent to about $100,000. In the summer of 1953 the administrative staff of the school was pleasantly surprised by the success of a fund-raising campaign which brought in almost 20,000,000 cruzeiros from Brazil. That much of that money was donated by United States business firms operating in São Paulo was viewed as a token of the esteem in which the school is held by the industrial community.

The administration of Mackenzie is in the hands of a board, a council, and a directorial staff. The board—a small group in New York that holds the title to the property—chooses the directors and holds veto power over the appointment of new members to the council. It has practically nothing to do with the direct management of the school. The fifteen-member council, including Catholics and Protestants, makes policy. All the councilmen live in Brazil, and only three or four of them claim United States citizenship. The president and treasurer of the school are United States Presbyterian missionaries, who draw salaries from the Mission Board and from the school itself. They assume few, if any, responsibilities in other activities of the Presbyterian church.

The industrialization of São Paulo removed old cultural values that might have impeded Mackenzie's program. New ideas and practices did not have to be wedged into a tradition-directed rural community. The rapid industrialization of the area has broken down the old class structure and thrown many time-honored social values to the winds. A modern, booming, industrial community places a premium on individual skill and competence and has little regard for the social status of workers, engineers, accountants, and business executives. The rise of a significant middle class in the area—a direct concomitant of the growing industrialization—has created demand for commercial and industrial training. Therefore, Mackenzie developed self-sustaining schools and courses in the commercial arts and applied sciences—an opportunity not available to missionary schools in many other areas.

The farsighted wisdom of Mackenzie's administrative staff has also been of profound importance in its growth and creativeness. One of its early presidents saw the need for an engineering school in the early 1890's and opened the first such private school in Brazil. This act, before the era of São Paulo's industrial boom, is excellent testimony to the wisdom, creativeness, and self-devotion of the president, who had a long and distinguished career at Mackenzie.

The combination of environment in change and able, farsighted leadership in control of a well-established educational institution has rarely been experienced by religious agencies in Latin America. As the next two cases indicate, however, the area of opportunity is wide.

COLEGIO SAN JOSÉ (BLUEFIELDS, NICARAGUA)

In Bluefields, a town of almost 7,500 people on the east coast of Nicaragua, there are three schools sponsored by outside religious agencies. One of these, Colegio San José, is under the general supervision of the Catholic bishop for the area and is operated by a group of Christian Brothers from the United States. The bishop, whose vicarate includes the whole east coast of Nicaragua, is a citizen of the United States and a member of the

Capuchin order. There are several Capuchin priests from the United States serving in his vicarate.

The east coast of Nicaragua is one of the few areas in any of the independent countries of Latin America in which a majority of the population is Protestant. There is a great mixture of races and nationalities along the east coast—a tropical rain forest area—but predominantly the present population of the coastal towns and river ports is of English-speaking Negro stock from the West Indies. In the surrounding jungle, however, are many Indians, who are descendants of the original inhabitants. Spanish-speaking mestizos from the west coast and central highlands of Nicaragua have migrated to the east coast in significant numbers within the last fifty years, and there is also a sprinkling of Chinese, Germans, and Swedes.

The Moravian church of Germany sent the first foreign missionaries to the area in 1849 to convert the Indians. During World War I, their activities were taken over by the Moravian church of the United States, which has continued to support a sizable group of missionaries along the east coast. They operate several schools and one hospital and tend small, scattered congregations. Though Moravians form the largest percentage of churchgoers, there are also Church of England Anglicans. In the town of Bluefields about one-third of the people are Catholic, and the proportion is probably the same in other east-coast towns and villages.

In some respects, therefore, the status of the Catholic missionaries in this area is analogous to that of Protestants in most of Latin America. They are working as a minority group among people of other faiths. The Capuchins from the United States have been in the area only about fifteen years, and apparently there was not much Catholic activity along the east coast before their arrival. In addition to Colegio San José, they now have numerous primary schools and clinics in the vicarate, some of which are operated by Maryknoll nuns from the United States.

San José is a boys' school, which was started in 1944. It was operated for one year under the direction of the bishop, with lay teachers. By 1945, the bishop had worked out a contract with the Christian Brothers for managing the school. During the first year of this arrangement, there were four Brothers and nine lay teachers. In 1953, the staff had changed to eleven Brothers and four lay teachers. At that time the Colegio was mainly a primary school with only two years of work above the sixth grade. Most of the students were being taught all their subjects by Christian Brothers from the United States, a rare arrangement in view of the fact that most of the schools operated by religious agencies employ nationals of the country in which they are located.

In the primary grades—the first six years of study—the school follows the curriculum required by Nicaragua. This is mainly reading, writing, and arithmetic, with some elementary work in history, geography, hygiene, civics, and drawing, taught in Spanish. The two years of secondary school meet the traditional requirements during day sessions, but there is a special commercial course taught in evenings and on week ends, so that boys who are working at full-time jobs can study English, bookkeeping, and typing.

In 1953, a total of 452 boys was enrolled in Colegio San José. Of these, 390 were in the primary grades and 62 in secondary. Fourteen of the latter were taking the commercial course. Present plans call for the addition of a secondary grade each year until there are five years of work above the primary level. This will make Colegio San José a full-fledged primary and secondary school which fulfils all governmental requirements for educational institutions of this type. There are no tuition charges or fees for students in the primary grades. The tuition is about $1.00 per month at the secondary level, but students are not turned away if they cannot pay. It is a school, therefore, available to the children of very poor families. All races and all denominations attend.

Perhaps the most significant thing about Colegio San José, besides the high quality of its staff, is the large number of extracurricular activities, including special vocational training for a portion of the students. For instance, the school sustains a seventy-piece band, an orchestra of 22 boys, a choir with 85 members, a Boy Scout troop, and an extensive athletic program after school hours. In addition to the vocational courses mentioned, there is a printing-shop, in which 5 or 6 boys are learning the printer's trade, and a carpentry shop for regular classes in woodworking. A member of the school staff operates a "ham" radio station that serves as a focal point around which a few boys are taught the rudimentary principles of radio transmission and reception. Another staff member has a small photography shop, where he teaches some boys how to do photographic work.

These various activities are of more than ordinary importance because of the peculiar nature of Bluefields. At one time, Bluefields was the administrative and shipping center of the United Fruit Company's banana operations in Nicaragua. Several years ago, however, the company abandoned banana production in the area because of a disease which attacks the roots of the banana trees. Bluefields had many of the characteristics of a "ghost town" until people began to grow African palm nuts on the deserted banana lands and the government started to build a road connecting the east and west coasts of Nicaragua. However, there are many unemployed, or seriously underemployed, people. Almost everybody is desperately poor; opportunities are so scant and the isolation so great that hopes for personal advancement have faded. This is a deadening environment for the vigor of youth, which needs more outlets than walking the streets of a half-deserted town and spinning daydreams that turn into haunting frustrations.

The Christian Brothers, a young, energetic group of North Americans, with their teaching, their extracurricular activities, their vocational classes, and their willingness to share hobbies, have brought a breath of fresh life to Bluefields. When their schoolboy band, its members dressed in cast-off uniforms sent down from schools in the States, parades to the airport to meet a visiting dignitary or, on rare occasions, is flown to the capital city of Managua to take part in a special celebration, it does more than create music. It provides a real and important psychological lift to a group of "dead-end kids." The carpentry shop provides a welcome relief from the tedium of the classroom, and learning the printer's trade may open the doors to a job away from the sterile influence of a decaying town surrounded by jungle.

The extracurricular activities and vocational training at San José are possible largely because the curriculum set forth by Nicaragua is not too exhaustive. After five or six hours of regular classwork, there is still plenty of time during the day for other activities. The climate is always warm, and the hours of daylight do not vary much from one time of the year to another, because Bluefields is only about 800 miles from the Equator. The school is situated on one of the main residential streets in a town of about 7,500. Most of the children can walk from their homes to the school in five or ten minutes. Hence the total environment makes it easy and natural for the school to become a center of youth activities. Over a period of years, it will unquestionably be an important and valuable influence on the lives of many children. In relation to the near-by Moravian school, which is larger and older, it appears to have an advantage, particularly in its appeal to children, because of its young and vigorous staff, its wide program of activities and vocational subjects, and the fact that it charges no tuition for the first six years.

Its one obvious weakness is the deficiency of agricultural knowledge among its staff members and the consequent lack of gardening or agricultural activities that could have an immediate influence on levels of living in the area. The particular group of Christian Brothers who operate this school, like most Catholic missionaries from the United States, have urban backgrounds. They are sufficiently skilled in music, photography, carpentry, and printing to be excellent teachers of young boys. Unfortunately, they know little about agriculture, even the primitive, jungle-type farming around Bluefields. Almost every family in the town could work a garden plot, and many of them have sufficient unemployed manpower to clear 2 or 3 hectares of jungle land for food crops. Farming in the jungle is not easy, and on any sizable commercial scale it probably would require capital and skill far beyond those of most residents. As a subsistence venture, however, it holds real possibilities for improving nutrition. If the staff of Colegio San José employed just one person skilled in the practical aspects of gardening and subsistence farming, he could encourage older boys in enterprises which, if they did not produce a small income for the students from the local sale of fruits and vegetables, would surely enhance the scant local food supply.

INSTITUTO RURAL EVANGÉLICO (ITAPINA, BRAZIL)

The Rural Evangelical Institute, sponsored by the Methodist church, is situated in an isolated rural area about 5 miles from the little town of Itapina, about 300 miles from Rio de Janeiro, in the state of Espírito Santo. The school was started in 1946 on approximately 100 acres of abandoned land, on which there were a few old coffee trees, a set of dilapidated farm buildings, and a good spring and reservoir, with sufficient water to irrigate a few acres of truck crops. In the summer of 1953, an additional 100 acres of land was purchased. Tentative plans call for this post to become a complete rural service center.

At the present time, the institute operates two primary schools, one for boarding students and the other for the children of neighboring farmers. The staff is beginning an agricultural extension service and maintains a few acres of field crops, an extensive garden, a herd of cattle, and a few hogs.[2] The farming and gardening activities only supply food for the stu-

2. The agricultural extension service is little more than a rural wholesale business that may develop into a co-operative. About twenty farmers bring eggs, citrus fruit, and other perishables for the agricultural missionary to take to market for them on the one day each week when he goes to town. The institute charges

dents and staff. The primary school for children of the neighborhood is operated like other Brazilian schools of this type, with most of the teachers' salaries paid by the government.

The boarding-school, on the other hand, is quite an unusual institution. It has about 50 students, both boys and girls, most of whom are fifteen years of age or older. They come from extremely poor farm families, and few of them have received any schooling before they arrive at the institute. It is common to see teen-age youngsters in the first of the five grades. Most of the students are Protestants referred to the institute by Brazilian pastors of rural Methodist and Presbyterian churches.

The curriculum of the boarding-school does not conform to governmental standards; therefore, it is neither accredited nor inspected. In the first and second years the principal subjects are Portuguese, world history, arithmetic, geography, science, art, and vocational agriculture for boys and home economics for girls. In the third and fourth years, Brazilian history is substituted for world history, and a course in civics is added. In the fifth and final year a course in the study of the Bible is added.

The academic subjects are taught by one full-time and two half-time Brazilian teachers who are graduates of secondary schools or colleges sponsored by the Methodist church elsewhere in Brazil. The courses in vocational agriculture, home economics, and Bible are taught by the three Methodist missionaries stationed at the institute. The man who teaches agriculture, manages the farm, and runs the little extension program for the benefit of neighboring farmers was not formally trained in agriculture, but he was reared on a Texas dairy farm. The home economics teacher is a graduate home economist.

The courses in agriculture and home economics are extremely practical: boys work on the farm four hours per day, and girls spend an equal amount of time working in the kitchen and dormitories. Much of their classwork is directly related to the jobs that they perform daily. Buildings and facilities, all of which are crude but quite in keeping with the local style, have either been constructed by student labor from bricks and tile made at the school or been repaired by the students with local materials. Nearly all the food consumed by the students and staff, who eat together in one dining hall, is produced on the farm. The meals are substantial and, because of a large

-----

a 10 per cent service fee for this marketing service. It also carries a small stock of seeds and insecticides for spraying cattle, killing ants, and similar purposes, which it sells to farmers at cost plus a small markup for transportation.

irrigated garden, usually well balanced. The daily menu is determined by what is available from the farm and garden. The traditional black beans and rice are the staple items, just as they are in millions of Brazilian homes because they can be grown and stored easily, but meat and green vegetables are added.

Life around the institute is hard. With four or five hours of classes, four hours of work on the farm or in the kitchen, two hours of study hall, rooms to be cleaned and laundry to be done, the day's activities start before the sun is up and end well after dark. In the dry season the dust is thick, and when it rains the mud is deep. If the weather does not permit work in the fields, there are buildings and fences to be repaired or new ones to be built. Abandoned fields have to be cleared and seeded to pasture or made ready for crops. The cattle have to be sprayed for ticks, and the pigs have to be fed, vaccinated, and wormed. Everybody works—faculty and students alike. There are no vows of poverty, but the environment hardly necessitates overt acts of self-negation.

Until 1953, the students paid only a matriculation fee of 100 cruzeiros per year, which equaled less than $5.00. In 1953, however, an additional tuition charge of 1,000 cruzeiros per year (then equivalent to about $25) was collected. Many of the students receive scholarships from the institute or from church organizations in Brazil which pay a part of their tuition. All other costs are covered by their work at the school. The Foreign Mission Board of the Methodist church puts up less than $10,000 per year for salaries, scholarships, and other operating costs. Its total investment in the land and physical facilities is approximately $30,000. Many of the students live on a higher level at the institute than they would at home, but this is a reflection of the poverty of their families rather than an indication of anything "fancy" at the institute.

In all respects this is an inexpensive rural school for children of poor farm families. Its location, physical facilities, courses, and teaching methods are part and parcel of the rural environment of Brazil. Five years of training, coming so late in life that many of the students are grown men and women when they graduate, does not produce many community leaders. Moreover, farming practices and the training courses in agriculture obviously could be improved. A well-trained, practical agriculturist could make an outstanding contribution. Nevertheless, this is a type of school needed by the thousands in Latin America. It is demonstrating a pattern that, if widely and wisely followed, could enrich rural life immeasurably.

ORT[3] VOCATIONAL CENTER (RIO DE JANEIRO, BRAZIL)

A small technical school, now financed entirely by the local ORT Brazilian Jewish Society, was started in 1943 with assistance from the American ORT Federation and continued to receive help from this source for three or four years. In 1953 it had an enrolment of 70 boys and 30 girls. Students of all races and creeds are admitted, but most of them belong to Jewish workingmen's families in Rio. A few are from Catholic families.

The school, called the "ORT Vocational Center," does not charge tuition or fees of any kind. It not only offers excellent training but also provides lunches and uniforms, as well as dental and medical care for all students. The basic curriculum is a four-year course for students thirteen to twenty years of age who have finished the first four grades. In other words, it is for students who have finished a standard primary school in Brazil.

The school day begins at seven o'clock in the morning and ends at five in the afternoon. This arrangement permits both parents of many of the children to have a full-time job while their youngsters are well cared for during the day. It also enables the students to take a technical course and at the same time do most of the work required in an ordinary junior high school (*Ginasio*).

The boys spend 15–18 hours per week in the machine shop, work 6 hours in design and mechanical drawing, and 1 hour in applied physics— a total of 22–25 hours in technical subjects. In addition, they pass 17 hours weekly in regular junior high subjects, such as Portuguese, natural science, geography, history, and physical education. Those of Jewish parentage have 4 hours per week in the study of Hebrew history and language. The curriculum is the same for girls, except that they are taught sewing and dressmaking while the boys are in the shop.

There are fifteen teachers on the faculty, most of whom are Brazilians serving on a part-time basis. The three teachers of shopwork and technical subjects are former citizens of Germany, who left that country during the Hitler regime. They are highly skilled technicians, and their students are probably better trained in machine-shop work than the graduates of any comparable school in Brazil.

Seventy-five students have graduated from the school since 1945. Of this

3. The ORT (Organization for Rehabilitation through Training) is an international organization, but its American unit has essentially the same autonomy as other religious agencies.

number, 15 have continued their education at the National Technical School in Rio, and 1 has become a teacher in that school. Most graduates are employed by industrial firms in the Rio area. Their salaries, at the time of employment in such firms, range from 2,000 to 3,000 cruzeiros per month—equivalent to about $50–$75 at 1953 rates of exchange.

A fairly good salary for graduates does not attract many students to ORT. It has buildings and facilities for 150 students but rarely enrols more than 75. A part of the difficulty appears to stem from management policies. The fact that the school is completely free, has been supported for the past few years mainly by professional and business members of the Rio Jewish community, and has centered attention on assisting Jewish students gives it the flavor of a charity for a particular group. There is great loyalty and interest on the part of the few people who make up its governing board and its fund-raising committee. To some it apparently serves as an important outlet for philanthropic motives toward less fortunate members of their religious group. The school's future success may depend on gaining a wider base of popular support. Financing the school is already a serious problem. Similar institutions have failed in São Paulo, Brazil, and Santiago, Chile, because they have been too much of a financial drain on a few loyal supporters. The school in Rio is unquestionably training students in the kind of knowledge and skills which Brazil needs. If it can broaden its horizons beyond that of providing a highly desirable charitable service to children of Jewish families and if it can serve all elements of the population on a basis assuring financial strength, it should be able to continue its effort.

Mackenzie Institute, San José College, Rural Evangelical Institute, and the ORT Vocational Center are institutions that have broken away from traditional patterns and methods. Only one of them, Mackenzie Institute, is of such size and age as to have become really significant in its environment. The others are small, young, and heavily dependent on their sponsors. They are all aiming at a new kind of education for Latin America. Mackenzie, which is in the center of the greatest industrial area of Latin America, has prospered, but the others have not found the means for self-support. At least two of them, San José College and the Rural Evangelical Institute, could be a great deal more effective if they added a well-trained agriculturist to their teaching staffs.

Paradoxically, schools of this type benefit those classes most which can pay least to support them. Technical and vocational schools are expensive to equip and more costly to operate than the ordinary primary and secondary institution. At the same time, they appeal to the lower-income classes in society—the group least able to pay for their children's education. In technical schools the religious agencies may serve a segment of the population which customarily receives little from Latin-American governments. If, however, the agencies increase their support of technical and vocational institutions, they will either have to get more money from the United States or reduce the number of institutions which they are sponsoring. This is the crux of their problem. If they move in the direction of greatest service to the poorer classes of Latin America, of inculcating the particular types of knowledge and skill in which the United States excels, and of providing leadership to the educational system of Latin America, they will unquestionably put a greater proportion of their effort into the type of work being done by Mackenzie Institute, San José College, Rural Evangelical Institute, and the ORT Vocational Center.

Health Activities

Most medical and health activities of United States religious agencies in Latin America are of three principal types: (1) fairly large urban hospitals, many of which have affiliated nursing schools; (2) small clinics and treatment-rooms in working-class districts of larger cities; and (3) small hospitals or clinics in rural mission posts, where there is usually a group of related activities, such as a primary school, a farm, and an agricultural extension service. The latter type of health program can best be described in the section of this chapter dealing with agricultural activities. The four cases reviewed here, therefore, show a fairly typical urban hospital with nursing school, a small urban clinic, a specialized maternity hospital, and an unusual health education program carried out by radio and mail. The latter case is by no means typical; it is an unusual attempt to reach a large audience with a few helpful hints about ways and means of improving health.

HOSPITAL BAUTISTA (MANAGUA, NICARAGUA)

The Baptist Hospital, situated in the outskirts of Managua is quite typical of urban hospitals operated by United States religious agencies in many of the larger cities of Latin America. This hospital was first opened in 1930 in a reconditioned building which had previously been used as living quarters for army officers. The property is owned by the Woman's American Baptist Home Mission Society, the sponsoring agency for the hospital.

The medical staff in 1953 was made up of one doctor from the United States, who was the director, and four Nicaraguan doctors, three of whom were employed on a salary basis. The other, the assistant director of the hospital, received a salary and was also allowed to accept fees from some of his patients. There were six or eight other private physicians in Managua who practiced at the Baptist Hospital. Usually five to ten beds were occupied by patients of these physicians.

There were forty-two beds in the hospital and three classes of service: (1) private rooms, for which patients payed approximately $6.00–$8.00 per day; (2) three- and four-bed wards, in which the charge per patient was approximately $3.50 per day; and (3) eight- and ten-bed wards, in which the per patient charge was approximately $2.00 per day. There were ten private rooms, four three- and four-bed wards, and two large wards. Room, food, nursing care, and medical dressings are covered by the regular fee; the cost of surgery, anesthetics, and medicines was extra. Patients in the private rooms and small wards were charged regular professional fees for the services of attending physicians. Patients in the eight- and ten-bed wards who were able to pay were also charged for the services of physicians. Many of them, however, were charity cases, who paid very little for the services of physicians, and some of them were not able to pay the hospital charges. In addition to the treatment and care of hospital patients, there was a regular weekly series of outpatient clinics. One of these was held at 8:30 every morning for low-income people, who pay little or nothing.

The hospital, however, is largely self-supporting. In addition to the salary of the director, who is a medical missionary, the sponsoring agency provides only about $4,200 per year in support of hospital activities.[4] Until 1942, the hospital centered its attention primarily on charity work, and the doctor from the United States devoted about 60 per cent of his time to surgery. During World War II while he served in the United States Army, the hospital was without a North American doctor on its staff. When he returned to his post at the end of the war, he found the hospital in serious financial difficulties. It was to meet this situation that he added Nicaraguan

4. This does not include a contribution of $6,000 per year to the nursing school.

doctors to the staff and began accepting patients in private rooms and small wards and charging them enough to cover most of the cost of the charity work.

Recently 850–900 people were admitted to the hospital each year. An average number of 25–30 patients occupy the hospital at any one time. In 1952, there were 358 operations at the hospital, of which 226 involved major surgery; in 1951 the respective totals were 469 and 295. There are usually from 125 to 150 babies born at the hospital each year. Between 6,500 and 7,000 patients per year are served at the clinics, which involve from 14,000 to 16,000 consultations.

TABLE 11

CURRICULUM OF NURSING SCHOOL IN HOSPITAL BAUTISTA

FIRST YEAR

Preliminary course (five months)

	Total Hours
Anatomy and physiology	80
Microbiology	45
Chemistry	45
History of nursing	20
Introductory ethics	15
Psychology	30
Personal hygiene	10
Dietetics and cooking	35
Elementary pharmacology and therapeutics	35
Elementary nursing practice	140
Supervised practice	240
Hospital economics	10
Physical education	5
Bandaging	10

Second part (three months)

	Hours per Month
Anatomy and physiology	25
Medical pathology	45
Surgical pathology	35
Operating-room technique	9

	Hours per Month
Advanced pharmacology and therapeutics	35
Advanced dietetics	20
Massage	16
Advanced nursing practice	50
Anesthesia	5

SECOND YEAR (NINE MONTHS)

Contagious diseases and immunology	30
Obstetrics	35
Pediatrics	28
Neurology and psychiatry	30
Gynecology	15
Urology	6
Orthopedics	10
Outpatient service*	

THIRD YEAR (NINE MONTHS)

Public health	20
Dermatology	10
Case observation	6
Eye, ear, nose, and throat	15
First aid	10
Advanced ethics	10
Occupational therapy	6
Outpatient service*	

* One month of practice for period of each clinic.

There are only two types of religious activity carried on in connection with the work of the hospital. A "Bible woman" is allowed to go through the wards to hand out religious literature to the patients. On request, she will also read the Bible or other religious literature to a patient. In addition, there is a short religious service, usually Bible reading and prayer, in the waiting-room for patients at the early morning clinic. This service has to be finished before 8:30 each morning, at which time the doctors start their consultations with clinic patients.

An important adjunct to the hospital is a nursing school, started in 1943. It is under the direction of a registered nurse from the United States, who, like the head of the hospital, is a salaried missionary of the sponsoring agency. The society contributes $6,000 per year toward the operating costs of the school. When the nursing school first opened, students were selected from graduates of the sixth-grade primary schools in Nicaragua. Admission standards have subsequently been raised so that student nurses must now have at least two years of secondary-school work before they are admitted. Moreover, they must be at least eighteen years old. Many of the new students are, in fact, high-school graduates.

The nursing course lasts for three school years of nine months each. Ten new students are admitted each year, of whom 2 or 3 usually drop out within the first six months. Thus there are usually from 20 to 30 girls in the student body, about one-third of whom are Protestant and the rest Catholic. From the inception of the nursing school in 1943 through 1953, there had been 42 graduates, at least 25 of whom were unmarried and practicing their profession, and 19 of whom were in Nicaragua; others have gone to Honduras, Mexico, Venezuela, Panama, El Salvador, and the United States. One graduate headed the national nursing school, and many graduates work at the municipal hospital in Managua.

Both the hospital and the nursing school are recognized as excellent medical institutions by the government and the community. North Americans in Managua patronize the hospital and its clinics when they need medical care, but most of its patients are Nicaraguans. A new hospital building was being constructed, with funds from the sponsoring agency, on a lot adjacent to the present building. When the new hospital is completed, total patient capacity will be almost doubled, and facilities for the care of patients will be greatly improved and modernized.

CLÍNICA ADVENTISTA (ASUNCIÓN, PARAGUAY)

The Seventh Day Adventists maintain a small clinic on the edge of the business district of Asunción. It is reasonably typical of one kind of medical institution sponsored by religious agencies in Latin America. Located in a small building of the sort commonly used for retail stores, it is arranged with a waiting-room in the front of the building and four or five small treatment-rooms in the rear. The responsible medical director of the clinic is a Paraguayan doctor whose duties are non-medical. The functioning staff from the inception of the clinic in 1946 until August, 1953, when a doctor from the United States was expected to arrive, included Argentinian and Chilean nurses and an Adventist missionary of Swedish nationality, who served as pastor of the Adventist church and administrative officer for the Paraguayan mission post. There are no more than three nurses on the staff, and one or two of them may be part-time employees.

Most of the patients treated at the clinic are sent by local doctors. The majority come for inoculations and injections of various types. In Asunción, as in many Latin-American cities, the ordinary practicing physician rarely gives injections himself. He writes a prescription, and the patient goes to a drugstore or clinic, where a licensed nurse or technician administers the "shot." This Adventist clinic also emphasizes physical therapy in the form of massages and heat treatments.

The clinic ordinarily treats from 3,000 to 3,500 patients a year, about 40 per cent of whom are from working-class families. Most of the others are from middle-income groups. Even the poorer patients are usually charged enough to cover half the cost of medicines. The fees charged those able to pay are sufficiently high that not more than 20 per cent of the annual budget of approximately $5,000 has to be contributed by the mission post.

MADRE E HIJO HOSPITAL (SANTIAGO, CHILE)

Mother and Child Hospital, situated in a semi-industrial area, is a small maternity hospital which was sponsored by the Presbyterian church in the United States until it was transferred to the Chilean Presbyterians in 1954. Started in 1927 as a small dispensary, it has grown to the point where it occupies two small buildings with nineteen beds and the necessary laboratory and delivery-room equipment for an efficient maternity hospital. Its physical growth resulted largely from gifts by individuals in the United States and Chile.

The director of the hospital, who has been transferred, was a registered American nurse and a medical missionary of the Presbyterian Board of Foreign Missions. Until 1952, she had an assistant who was also a registered nurse and a missionary from the United States, but after that she was the only North American connected with the hospital. Her regular staff consists of three trained midwives and six nurse's aids. Two doctors—one an obstetrician, the other a pediatrician—give part of their time to the hospital. The midwives take care of all normal deliveries, and the obstetrician is called only for problem cases. There is also a follow-up pediatric program for children born in the hospital.

Prenatal clinics are held as study groups. Any married woman is eligible to attend these clinics and have her baby delivered in the hospital if she enrols not later than the fifth month of pregnancy. Each study group meets once a month with a nurse, who delivers well-planned lessons and presides over discussions. Brief private consultations with the individual mothers follow. Prenatal clinics in the form of discussion groups enable the hospital to handle a large number of cases, at the same time educating women in personal hygiene, proper diet, and home sanitation. The private consultations permit the nurse to examine the individual patients, advise them of any special problems which they may expect to have in connection with the birth of their children, and to decide which women should be attended at the time of delivery by the obstetrician instead of a midwife.

The hospital also conducts a series of pediatric clinics in the form of discussion groups to which each mother is encouraged to return with her child for a monthly lecture and examination until the child is six years old. Nearly all the mothers come faithfully until their children are about three years old, but only a quarter of them attend regularly after that. Besides advising mothers on child care and nutrition at these clinics, the hospital staff inoculates the children against common diseases. Though the pediatrician seldom appears for a clinic, he may be consulted in a difficult case.

The mostly lower-middle-class women served by the hospital are able to pay the fee of 1,500 pesos (equivalent to approximately $9.00 in 1953) for medical attendance and six days' care, and they are charged 20 pesos for each prenatal clinic. Their money, plus the income from two expensive private rooms, meets the hospital's current operating expenses. Capital improvements and some medicines have been paid for by a Patroness Committee of Chilean and a few North American women which raises funds. The annual budget, 2,000,000 pesos, was equivalent to approximately

$12,500 in 1953. Before the transfer to Chilean ownership the Board of Foreign Missions paid only the salary of the director.

Respected by the community and the nation, the hospital has delivered 11,000 babies, and the director has been decorated by the government. It is a prime example of an institution meeting a widespread need well.

The three preceding examples typify medical programs sponsored by religious agencies in urban areas of Latin America. The basic core of their work is treatment, inoculation, and hospitalization. In the larger hospitals, such as the one in Managua, all activities are carried out in one institution. A majority of the large urban hospitals sponsored by the agencies have inaugurated nursing schools if for no other reason than to be assured of good nursing service for their patients.

The professional competence of the doctors and nurses on the staff of these institutions is uniformly high. The medical missionaries are nearly always better trained in their profession than other types of missionaries engaged in technical work. Among doctors, however, the skill of those representing religious agencies is probably no better than, and in some cases not so good as, the best 25 or 30 per cent of native doctors. This does not mean that the agency doctors are inferior practitioners; instead, it indicates the high medical standards in Latin America and the excellence of local practitioners. Most of the best ones practice in the larger cities, where they give adequate care to patients who can afford their services. The nursing profession, on the other hand, is not highly developed in Latin-American countries. Nurses trained in the United States are professionally competent to assume more responsibility in caring for patients than locally trained nurses are.

Seldom have missionaries introduced distinctly new or improved methods and techniques of medical practice, but there is evidence that their hospitals and clinics have stimulated governments and private doctors to serve low-income families. For instance, it was only a year or two after the Baptist Hospital in Managua opened that the local medical society began a series of regular clinics for charity cases. Within another few years, a large municipal hospital, financed by the national government, was serving patients of the same type as those who commonly come to the Baptist Hospital.

It is not unusual for a missionary hospital to be a focal point where local doctors meet and discuss medical problems or where special work in animal surgery or some similar activity increases the skill and competence of local doctors. Medical students in near-by universities are sometimes given special opportunities to observe cases with the doctors who practice at the hospitals of the religious agencies. All these activities tend to expand the influence of the medical work of the agencies beyond their institutional walls. Valuable as this work is in the larger and better-equipped urban hospitals, its total influence is not major.

The low state of personal hygiene and home sanitation has been little improved by the medical missionaries. This most obvious deficiency in the health program is apparent within a stone's throw of the Baptist Hospital in Managua, for example, where families are living in such filth and dirt that their bodies and their homes harbor disease and vermin. This kind of scene is duplicated in section after section in city after city. Urban slums in Latin America, overcrowded homes, lack of garbage disposal, inadequate water supplies and sewage facilities, high rates of disease and delinquency, resemble urban areas of blight and human misery in the United States.

Though several Latin-American governments have inaugurated programs of spraying homes and other buildings with the new insecticides, few, if any, of these programs have resulted from the work of medical missionaries. The hospitals and clinics of the agencies carry out important aspects of a program of preventive medicine by the numerous inoculations which they encourage their patients to take against common diseases; however, they have not reached large numbers of people with simple suggestions about how to keep well. The whole problem of personal hygiene and home sanitation is a complex one, with many social and economic implications that call for the teacher, the community-organization specialist, and the public information man, as much as the doctor.

One way in which the problem is being tackled by a religious agency is illustrated in the following case.

"THE VOICE OF THE HOME" RADIO PROGRAM (MEXICO)

Since 1945, the Inter-American Division of the General Conference of Seventh Day Adventists has been sponsoring in Mexico a weekly radio program concerned primarily with health problems. The use of the radio for evangelistic purposes is a well-established practice, but this is one of the few programs, if not the only one, in Latin America on which a religious agency has regularly broadcast health information to the public. By 1954, it had grown in popularity to the point where it was carried by about fifty stations reaching nearly the whole country. Each weekly program is prepared in Spanish in Mexico City, recorded, and mailed to the co-operating stations. Only ten of the fifty stations that customarily broadcast it are paid to do so. The others carry it as a free public service or find local sponsors.

The central theme of the program is "The Voice of the Home Brings Health and Happiness." Because religious broadcasts are banned in Mexico, the program contains no material of a specifically religious nature. Each broadcast advertises a free health correspondence course of sixteen lessons. Those who take the health correspondence course are encouraged by further advertisments to enrol in a Bible correspondence course, which is purely doctrinal in content. The radio program is justified by those interested in "soul-winning" as an important first step in a total project which is mainly evangelistic.

The radio program dramatizes everyday problems of ordinary people in their struggles to live healthfully and happily. In the early years of the program, its format was that of a lecture between renditions of the song "Home Sweet Home." When experience proved this documentary type of broadcast inffective in arousing listener interest, the format was changed to a dialogue type of "true-to-life" episodes in the fictional careers of two families. One was the "ideal family" of husband, wife, and two teen-age children, all happily adjusted and able to cope with their problems. The other was the "unhappy family" of husband, pregnant wife, and three children, all of whom were constantly in trouble with themselves and their environment. The cast included "the family doctor" and "the community nurse," characters meant to give authority to the medical advice. This general type of format was continued for about seven years, then was replaced by the simpler family counselor—an elderly man who answers health questions and explains the functioning of the human body. This format is much plainer than the one which preceded it, but it loses some of the values of contrast and comedy that could be created easily with the two-family cast.

Most of the programs explicate some specific aspect of such subjects as personal hygiene, first aid, home nursing, healthful diet, and basic morality. All scripts are approved by the secretary of health before they are recorded, and they are based on materials prepared by the Medical Department of

the General Conference of Seventh Day Adventists. Scripts and recordings
are done by a specialist who is an Adventist missionary stationed in Mexico
City. The following programs were broadcast in the latter part of 1953
and early 1954: "Sickness in the Home," "The Good Breakfast," "Child
Care," "The Importance of Bathing," "Diet and Exercise," "Can Cancer
Be Cured?" "How To Live Well," "The Value of Money," "School Days,"
"Matrimony," "Sleep," and "The River of Life."

A review of several scripts indicated that a remarkable amount of practical advice about ways and means of living healthfully was woven into
the broadcasts. Much of the material was of the same general type as that
which appears in family magazines in the United States or is broadcast by
extension services and public health departments. Its very generality ex-
cludes the pinpoint type of specificity that may be necessary in coping
with the health and sanitation problems that confront most Latin-American families. This, of course, is a common weakness of radio programs designed to serve families living in widely different situations. Nevertheless,
mass dissemination of medical information is worthy of serious consideration by other religious agencies. By reaching the many, it keeps some well,
thus complementing any health program which emphasizes the treatment
of patients after they are already sick. The total cost of the Adventist venture, including the salary of the director, is less than $15,000 per year to the
sponsoring agency. This is about the amount of money, exclusive of the
cost of buildings and equipment, that an agency customarily puts into the
operation of an urban hospital and nursing school in a Latin-American city.

In addition to the educational value of the radio program, it is an important advertising medium for the health correspondence course. From
1945 through December, 1953, almost 20,000 students had enrolled in the
course. Over 6,600 had graduated—finished the sixteen required lessons—
and received their diplomas. There were over 2,000 active students in this
course in 1953. Prepared by the same department and approved by the
same bureau that deal with the broadcasts, the lessons are aimed at giving
the student an elementary background in human physiology. They teach
him how to recognize the need for a doctor, and they suggest ways and
means of keeping the body healthy.

Agricultural Programs

The agricultural work of religious agencies in rural areas of Latin
America is commonly organized around mission posts located on

farms. A mature rural program is usually made up of four components: a farm and agricultural extension service; a formal school or schools; a medical service; and an evangelistic ministry. Some of the rural missions maintain only two or three of these activities, but nearly all have a farm and some kind of school. The combining of agricultural, educational, medical, and evangelical activities into one rural program is an expression of the view that Christianity is interested in the "whole man." This approach also provides a convenient administrative way for several North American families to live and work together in an isolated rural environment.

Several rural programs in Ecuador, Peru, and Bolivia are aimed specifically at improving the lot of the Andean Indians. These Indians—numbering between six and eight million—are the descendants of the Inca civilization, which, before the Spanish conquest, had developed an excellent agricultural economy. After four centuries of exploitation, the Indians resist, in a sullen, ignorant, suspicious, and dogged manner, the encroachment of the white man's ideas.

At the present time many rural Indians are attached to large farms (haciendas), where they live in small houses that they have built on the few acres of land which provide their food crops. They are often required to work three to five days per week for the hacienda owner. Other Indian families live in villages, cultivate near-by units of land, and work part time as hired laborers on large farms or at unskilled jobs in the villages. Still others farm land owned by Indian communities, on rental terms determined by the community officials. Although numerous Indians are voluntarily transferring themselves to the orbit of Western culture by such methods as speaking Spanish, cutting their long hair, and wearing the white man's clothes, multitudes refuse to make the shift. Many of those who do take on the outward accouterments of Western civilization preserve a lingering suspicion of their former conquerors and a wary distrust of new ideas and practices.

It is the desire of missionaries in technical work in the Andean area to demonstrate that there are white people who love and respect the Indians and want to help them improve their level of living. The three following cases typify rural mission posts attacking the "Indian problem." Their methodology is common among the agencies in the Andes.

UNITED ANDEAN INDIAN MISSION (TABACUNDO, ECUADOR)[5]

The United Andean Indian Mission post is sponsored jointly by the foreign mission organizations of two Presbyterian churches, the Evangelical and Reformed church, and the Evangelical United Brethren church. Each of the four bodies is supposed to furnish two missionaries, to share equally in financing the mission, and to send representatives to the board of the United Andean Indian Mission, which has its headquarters in New York City. The original plans for the post called for one missionary couple to devote their time to agricultural activities, another to direct the educational work, a third to handle the medical program, and a fourth to assume responsibility for evangelistic activities.

As a matter of practice, the original plan for staffing the post has never been achieved. The program got under way in the spring of 1946, with one missionary couple—the evangelist and his wife—in the field. It was fifteen months before the next couple—an agriculturist and his wife—arrived on the scene. They left in the fall of 1952, only about a year after the medical missionary and his wife had arrived. An educational specialist had not yet been added to the staff by the summer of 1953, the date of the field visit. The evangelist, who also acted as administrative officer of the post, served in still a third job, namely, director of education. Despite the administrative and staffing problems, he has made some progress.

The post is located on a 400-acre hacienda in the highlands of Ecuador near the village of Tabacundo, which is about a four-hour drive by automobile from Quito. Almost in the center of the 400-acre tract are 22 Indian families who have gained ownership rights to farms of 2–5 acres each, which are located in such a manner that they cut the mission land into two separate holdings. An important objective of the program is to gain the confidence and respect of these Indian families. Their expanded farms and improved health, education, and income are meant to be object lessons in solving the Indian problem. At the same time, it is hoped that some will become such good farmers, good Christians, and good community leaders that they can go into other areas and aid their own people. These are ambitious objectives; at the end of seven years little had been done toward their achievement.

5. This mission post is a direct outgrowth of an excellent report entitled *Indians of the High Andes*, edited by Dr. W. Stanley Rycroft, written by a five-man commission of experienced missionaries and published by the Committee on Co-operation in Latin America in 1946.

The medical program was probably most advanced by the summer of 1953. It had started in 1946 with an Ecuadorian nurse and the part-time services of a local doctor. For the first five years it was little more than a program of dispensing simple medicines to large numbers of people and providing home nursing care to a limited number of patients. This was changed in 1951 soon after the missionary doctor from the United States arrived at the post. Within fifteen to eighteen months he had built a small clinic building with an operating room, dispensary, and laboratory. Adjoining the clinic are sanitary, Indian-type huts, where ten bed-patients may be accompanied by members of their families during their period of hospitalization. About 200 patients per month are treated at the clinic and hospital at the headquarters post. An additional 200 are treated each month in clinics held at neighboring villages. A nurse from the United States was added to the staff in 1953. This medical program appears to be important in gaining the confidence of the Indians, as well as in providing badly needed medical care. The charges for medical service are less than enough to pay for the medicines.

The educational program consists of a primary school, from the first through the sixth grades, and a small adult-training program. The primary school opened in 1946 with 5 pupils, under the direction of the wife of the evangelist. By 1952 it had grown to an enrolment of 43 pupils, most of whom were children of the Indian families living in the center of the mission hacienda. The school is now run by two Ecuadorian Protestant teachers. It offers the regular required courses for primary grades, together with a course in gardening for the boys, a sewing course for girls, and a class in religious instruction which meets twice each week. An important feature of the school is that the children are given both breakfast and lunch. This not only encourages attendance but is also an important step toward improving the diets of the children. Most of them come from the homes of Indians who rarely have enough to eat. The only payments made by the students total 2 sucres per month—an amount equal to about one day's wage for an Indian farm worker. The adult-education program is a class for Indian men which meets three times a week for one hour of instruction in reading and writing. The adult class expressly helps the Indians on the hacienda to qualify as voters, literacy being a voting requirement in Ecuador. At the end of three years, only 5 men had become qualified voters.

The agricultural program was at a low ebb in the summer of 1953. The agricultural missionary had made some progress in getting the farm equipped and improved, but very little had been done after his departure in the fall of 1952. Most of the land is extremely poor, and much of it is badly eroded. The need for land improvement and soil-conservation work is tremendous. The agricultural missionary had made a good start, before his departure, in reforestation, contour farming, and the seeding of improved pastures. He had also done a little plot demonstration work with types and varieties of crops that were new to the area. To improve the breed of local livestock, the mission imported a purebred Brown Swiss bull, two boars, one ram, and a purebred Loggenburg goat. A few Indian families brought their cows and sows to be bred by the sires, but the number was small. The Indians refused to use the services of the ram; yet the small flocks of sheep are the most important livestock enterprise that the Indians have.

In the summer of 1953, plans were being discussed to subdivide a part of the land of the hacienda and sell it at a very low price to Indians who would agree to improve their farming practices and modernize their floorless, windowless houses. Although a modest farm enlargement and tenure improvement program through distributing a part of the mission lands to the Indian families living on the hacienda was a part of the original plan, nothing specific had been accomplished by the end of the seventh year of operation. Indeed, it was difficult to see that any impact had been made on the farming and living practices of the Indians. The mission farm operations, though they supplied some of the food for the missionary families and the school lunch program, had consistently lost money.

The sponsoring agencies had invested about $30,000 in this post by 1953, and more capital was needed. Salaries and expenses fluctuated from year to year, but in 1952 they totaled about $14,000, making it clear that this mission post represents a relatively heavy investment in funds and manpower. By the end of its seventh year, the mission had developed a good medical program and a better-than-average rural primary school. Its agricultural work had suffered because of personnel turnover. The Indians are developing a growing confidence in the missionaries, but there is little evidence that the latter have yet cracked the wall of ignorance and suspicion that separates the two cultures.

RURAL BRETHREN MISSION (CALDERÓN, ECUADOR)

An enterprise similar to the one just described is sponsored by the Foreign Mission Commission of the Church of the Brethren. Located about

15 or 20 miles from Quito, near the village of Calderón, it was established in 1946 to help the Calderón Indians—a group of small farmers, many of whom now work in Quito several days a week while their wives and children do the farming. This group of Indians has a reputation for heavy drinking, poor farming, and petty thievery. Their traditional way of life has been disrupted by their nearness to a metropolitan area with a growing demand for labor. The soil of their little farms, most of which are less than 15 acres in size, is extremely poor and sandy.

The mission station of the Brethren involves three separate tracts of land totaling about 185 acres. On one tract are the headquarters buildings —three dwellings, barns, sheds, and light plant. On another tract about a mile away is an old hacienda house, now used as the mission school. The third tract is a small area of farm land which had to be purchased with the hacienda. It is rented to two Indian tenants. Most of the land is too hilly for farming, and the small areas which are reasonably level have sandy, light soil that can bear few crops.

The principal interests of the station are agriculture, education, health, and evangelism. The staff of three married couples, an unmarried nurse from the United States, and two Ecuadorian schoolteachers is directed by the evangelist. An agriculturist oversees the farming, and an educational director manages the two-teacher primary school of 50 pupils. The nurse dispenses medicines to the Indian families, does some home visiting, and assists a native doctor from Quito who is brought to the post one day a month to hold a clinic for the benefit of the neighboring families.

In the school regular courses required of accredited primary schools in Ecuador are taught by the native teachers. To these are added a course in gardening, taught by the agriculturist, one in shopwork, and one in Bible stories. The children are given a light breakfast and a good lunch at the school. For the gardening class, each boy has a small plot from which he can take vegetables to his family. The breakfast and lunch for the children in school, together with the garden vegetables for family consumption, are important contributions to the diets of those families with children in the school. The Ecuadorian teachers are reasonably well qualified for primary-school work, and it is probable that most of the Indian children enroled would not be receiving any type of formal training if it were not for the efforts of missionaries. The school, therefore, is a significant contribution to the welfare of this Indian community.

The agriculturist, an experienced missionary from China, had been at the station only about a year at the time of the field visit in the summer of 1953. He had not yet developed an extension program of any consequence among the Indian farmers. He had a few demonstration plots sown in new varieties of crops and a purebred bull, boar, and ram for service in the community. During the previous year 20 Indian families had brought sows to the boar, 10 farmers had bred cows to the bull, but only 1 had used the services of the ram. Most of the agriculturist's time was spent in producing food for the school lunch program and for the families on the staff. He had not yet decided what new practices, if any, could be safely recommended to the Indian farmers. He is conscious of the danger of changing their traditional methods before he is assured that his recommendations are sound and beneficial.

This lack of knowledge on which to base an extension program is partly a reflection of the lack of experience in the area on the part of the agriculturist. To some extent it is also a result of inadequate research and experimental work throughout Ecuador. Of even greater significance is the fact that the Calderóns are really part-time farmers, with very inadequate units for full-scale operations. Moreover, the soil is so poor and sandy that it would be next to impossible to produce a decent level of living short of a major farm-enlargement and land-development program that would necessitate large amounts of capital and displace many of the present families. The resulting complex farm units would present management problems far beyond the interest and experience of the Indian farmers.

Both the social and physical environments of the Calderón Indians suggest a program aimed at teaching the women and children some type of handicraft skills and at training the young men in trades that will pay them higher wages in the city. In other words, a purely agricultural extension program may be much less appropriate than the teaching of non-farm skills. The problem of Indian families farming poor soil is common to the Andean area, but rarely does an opportunity for city employment exist, as it does for the Calderóns. An experiment in adult vocational training of Indians to combine farming with city work could help untangle the whole problem.

In contrast to the well-developed program of medical care at the United Andean Indian Mission only a few miles away, the medical program of the Rural Brethren Mission is rather meager. The nurse has a treatment-room and dispensary, in and from which she aids near-by families. Much of her work is in the nature of "follow-up" to the clinic, held one day each month by an Ecuadorian doctor hired by the mission to examine and treat Indians who will come to his clinic.

Approximately $25,000 have been invested in the physical facilities of this post, and its annual operation costs the sponsoring agency almost $20,000. The staff and several part-time workmen probably do not reach more than 300 Indian families per year through combined health, school, and farm activities, and these families receive little more than simple medicines and some nursing care. Badly needed as these services are, there again is little evidence that the missionaries have gained the understanding and confidence of the Indians to the point where they are able to guide them into new, creative uses of their land and labor resources. There appears to be a great need for a program reaching into the homes of the Indian families and making the work of the women and children profitable while the men and older boys continue to work in the city.

OREGON FRIENDS FARM (COPAJIRA, BOLIVIA)

The Board of Missions of the Oregon Yearly Meeting of Friends supports a mission house and church in La Paz, 11 rural primary schools, about 25 churches with Bolivian pastors, and a large farm situated on the shore of Lake Titicaca. The farm contains 3,000 acres, one-third of which are tillable. It is operated as a commercial enterprise, and, in contrast to many mission farms, it has been quite profitable. Not only does it conduct a Bible school with an enrolment of 20–25 Indian boys, who are studying to become rural pastors, and a primary school for the children of Indian families, but a part of its earnings are used to pay salaries of teachers and pastors in near-by areas. Moreover, it provides an example of a land distribution program to Indian families, which is similar to that carried out by some other religious agencies in the Andean region.

The farm, purchased in 1947, produces principally potatoes, barley, oats, and wheat. It pastures about 1,000 head of sheep and a few cattle and hogs. Its acres and machinery are capably managed by an experienced farmer from Idaho. It is situated on the cold, barren *Altoplano*—a rough, treeless plain—at an altitude of 13,000–15,000 feet above sea-level in an area populated by Quechua- and Aymara-speaking Indians, most of whom live and work on large, privately owned haciendas.

Thirty Indian families lived on the mission farm at the time it was purchased by the Oregon Friends. Each family had a windowless, dirt-floored, adobe house, 3 or 4 acres of land for food crops, and pasture rights for a few sheep and cattle. As rent for these units, each family had to furnish four to five man-days of labor per week to the hacienda-owner. Most of this work was performed by the head of the household, in the form of field labor, but some women and older girls performed household duties in the owner's home. Children and women often herded sheep. This system has been a customary form of peonage in Bolivia and some other Latin-American countries for many years. For decades it has been the concern of several United States religious agencies to abolish it.

Apparently the first direct approach to altering this tenure system was made by the Canadian Baptists in the Lake Titicaca area almost forty years ago. The same pattern has since been adopted by other religious agencies, including the Oregon Friends. Their program of "giving the Indians their freedom" has been to offer each of the 30 Indian families on the hacienda title to 5–10 acres of land, provided that they would (1) work 100 days on the mission farm for each hectare of land that they purchased; (2) build new, painted houses, with windows, on a different area of the farm from that on which the Indian village was originally located; and (3) agree to follow the farming practices recommended by the agriculturist on the mission post.

By the summer of 1953, about three years after this offer had been made to the Indians, 23 families were residing in new houses and had become the owners of 5- to 10-acre farms. The remaining seven families did not want to move from their old village, located about one mile from the center of the new settlement, and therefore had refused the offer to become landowners. After meeting the terms of the purchase contract, the 23 families were no longer obligated to work on the mission farm. In practice, most of them worked part time for wages and several of them rented a few additional acres by paying in field labor.

This type of miniature land-reform program gives Indians farms about the same size and type as those to which they are accustomed, and it encourages them to build considerably better houses than those in which they have previously lived. At the same time, it frees the Indian from continued work for the landlord. He is able to pay for his land with a stated amount of labor—in this case, 100 man-days per hectare. When he has finished paying for his new and improved house, he receives title to his land without other obligation to his former landlord than to follow suggested farming practices—an obligation not legally enforceable. The procedure effectively breaks the bonds of peonage and has some influence in raising the level of living of the Indians. If there were other opportunities within the local area for the Indians to earn a livelihood by wagework for other employers, it could be a very significant step toward improving their situation. Since it is a practice not likely to be followed voluntarily by private landlords, it can hardly be considered a demonstration of a land-reform program that will affect major estates operated under inequitable tenure arrangements.

There is no evidence that the comprehensive land-reform law enacted by the Bolivian government in the summer of 1953 received any particular impetus from the work of the religious agencies. Nevertheless, the experiences of the Oregon Friends show that it is possible to operate a good farm on the *Altoplano* at a profit and to provide fair and equitable treatment to the Indian laborers. The Indians are certainly better off than when they were peons on the hacienda before it was purchased as a mission post. The profits from the farm support schools and churches in several communities. The Indian families have just set foot on the long road to efficient operation of their newly acquired farms.

The combined experiences of the three mission stations described in the immediately preceding pages represent a good cross-section of the work of United States religious agencies to improve the lot of the Andean Indians. They also illustrate the tremendous difficulties of the job to be done. In seven years of operation none of them had really pulled the Indians out of a primitive rut. Two of the stations— the United Andean Indian Mission and the Oregon Friends' Farm— centered attention on the Indian families at hand, although the former has a medical program in surrounding areas. Even the families on the farms, however, progressed haltingly toward higher levels of living. The land-distribution program of the Oregon Friends certainly has been an important step in the right direction (and landowner-ship may provide a necessary base on which to build an adult-education program), but land reform is a national problem. It will not be solved until it becomes a part of a positive, long-time policy of governments.

The schools on the three posts are giving instruction through the primary grades to a total of 125–50 Indian children who would otherwise not be in school. This commendable effort, like others, has not stimulated governments to increase the number of rural schools for Indian children. Neither has it demonstrated new approaches to the problem of educating Indian children. There is obviously a large and important gap between an Indian child finishing the sixth grade and the same child beginning a new and constructive lifework. To teach him to read and write is very much worth while. On the other hand, if he has no hope but to live with his illiterate family in a one- or two-room house shared with the rabbits, guinea pigs, chickens, dogs, and hogs and can look forward to no other prospect in life than tilling 5-10 acres of poor land, provided that he can somewhere find the land, his sixth-grade education has been of little significance to him. The religious agencies are cognizant of this problem. The Oregon Friends train rural pastors, drawing the pastoral candidates from the primary-school graduates. The United Andean Indian Mission has granted a few scholarships to Indian children who study at a government normal school near Quito.

Although the work which the agencies are doing is worthy of support and expansion, the task which they are facing is so large, complex, and difficult that other approaches merit attention. In areas where the population pressure is not too heavy and where there are fairly large numbers of independent Indian farmers, a broad, down-to-earth rural educational program for both adults and children might succeed. This would have to be a program touching almost *Fundamental* every phase of Indian life. It would focus on such objectives as *Education* teaching women and children home handicrafts, including weaving, sewing, knitting, and leather-work; teaching men and older boys how to obtain higher yields per acre and per head of livestock; teaching some of the younger men non-farm skills that would enable them to become carpenters, masons, pottery workers, weavers, and blacksmiths in their local communities and near-by towns or to migrate to the cities and obtain jobs above the level of freight porters and ditch diggers. Such a program would also lay emphasis on health, housing, and home sanitation and would teach reading, writing, and simple arithmetic to both children and adults.

Many missionaries are, to a limited extent and in a rather halting fashion, trying to make this type of approach to the problem. However, as is evident from the three cases reviewed, their work is far from comprehensive, not very imaginative, and not greatly successful. It is doubtful that they will effectively cope with the problem as long as they rely exclusively on North American personnel assisted by a few mestizo schoolteachers. Most members of the mission stations lack specific skills that must be taught to the Indians. The North Americans rarely learn the Indians' language in a really fluent, workaday manner, and they live in a world of ideas and values that is miles apart from that of the Indian. Mestizo schoolteachers consider themselves far above the Indians' status. Distrusted by the Indians, they are usually short of vocational skills and effective methods for teaching adults.

If the missionaries would use some of the skilled Indian workmen, who live in areas near mission stations, as teachers of other Indians, they would be taking a great step forward. Putting skilled Indians on the mission payrolls as part-time employees, giving them general guidance in their teaching work, and bringing them new ideas and techniques from time to time would make teachers and leaders for the Indian families served by the mission station.

A second approach to the Indian problem is that of resettlement. In the Andean countries the Indians are thickly concentrated in the highlands—many of them at altitudes of more than 10,000 feet above sea-level—while land goes undeveloped in the lowlands. There are tremendous problems to be solved, including threats to human health, in shifting families from the highlands to the jungles; nevertheless, there are possibilities of mission posts being located so that there is a purposeful working relationship between those in highland areas and others in the lowlands. Those Indian families for whom the change in altitude was not severe would probably move permanently to the lowlands if they were assured of good farms and assistance in getting started. It is quite feasible for relatively large numbers of other Indian workers to work for three or four months at a time in the lowlands and then return to their highland homes. Carefully planned and efficiently operated mission farms in the lowlands could provide employment opportunities for such migrants. Mission stations might also help Indian communities farm land in both highland and lowland areas by shifting different groups from the same community back and forth every two to four months.

A third approach to the Indian problem would involve the operation of small factories in the highlands and the training of Indians to become factory workers. If such an approach could be combined with a broad program of rural education and geared to the utilization of labor not efficiently employed on farms, it would offer much-needed economic opportunities and relieve some of the population pressure on the land. This approach may involve too much capital and specialized managerial skill to be sponsored by most religious agencies. However, it is not unreasonable for some mission posts to encourage weaving, needlework, and similar activities in Indian homes or small workshops by furnishing materials, providing patterns or designs, and acting as sales agents of the resulting products. The promotion of "cottage industries" may, in fact, be less risky to the sponsoring agency than farming.

None of the ways in which religious agencies can tackle the Andean Indian problem will be easy; neither will they bring quick and large-scale results. It is important that those agencies now wrestling with the problem realign their programs so as to include more activities than clinics, schools, and demonstration farms beyond imitation by the Indian farmers. Of even greater importance is the necessity for the missionaries to influence the daily routine of the Indian's life in hundreds of little ways and to win acceptance as persons who can understand his thoughts and values. The greatest handicap that the missionaries have to overcome in working with the highland Indians is the wall of ignorance, indifference, and suspicion that has been built up between the two cultures.

The medical activities and the programs of land distribution are of great importance in gaining the confidence of the Indians. They are not, however, being followed up with imaginative programs of teaching personal skills and improved agricultural practices that are usable and useful to the Indian farmer. Little is being done to capitalize on the Indians' love of fiestas, dancing, and group activities. A constructive educational approach to the Indians' need for recreation appears to be an excellent means by which the missionary can gain the confidence of the Indian. In many respects the ordinary Indian is a child, and numerous aspects of his behavior are more typical of six- to twelve-year-old children than of any other type we have in our society. In the child's life, play and fantasy are important. They can both be channeled in constructive directions.

The agricultural activities of religious agencies in Latin America are not, of course, limited to the difficult and time-consuming work with the highland Indians. Moreover, most of the programs have met with considerably greater success than those concerned primarily with the "Indian problem." One of the most outstanding and widely known rural mission stations in Latin America is described in the following case study.

EL VERGEL MISSION STATION (ANGOL, CHILE)

El Vergel, which in English means "The Flower Garden" or fully translated, "The Garden of Paradise," is a large, highly profitable, and efficiently managed farm that maintains an agricultural school for boys, a home economics school for girls, two primary schools for the children of families who live on the farm, a clinic for the farm workmen and their families, and a social center. The station was started in 1919 by the Foreign Mission Board of the Methodist church, which paid $275,000 for the 3,800-acre farm, on which there was then a prosperous nursery for the production of horticultural and ornamental plants. The farm has been self-supporting since its very first year as a mission post and has been the source of most of the funds invested in the educational facilities that are now connected with it.

The farming operations represent two distinct types of agriculture. Much of the farm is made up of rough, rolling, hill land, suitable mainly for pasture and forestry. Additional acreage of fertile valley land is adaptable to several crops. The major farm enterprises are a large commercial nursery, from which fruit trees and ornamental shrubs are shipped to all parts of Chile; extensive apple orchards; a sixty-cow dairy herd for the production of salable milk; a herd of registered hogs for the production of breeding stock; an extensive forest for the production of timber; and two cattle-fattening enterprises. The gross income of the farm in recent years has been equivalent to $80,000–$100,000 annually. The farm is widely known in agricultural circles in Chile as an excellent source of good nursery stock and as having demonstrated many new and improved practices in its orchards and forests. El Vergel will also be long remembered as the institution which introduced into Chile a wasplike insect that feeds on the larvae of the woolly aphis, a parasite that was doing great damage to commercial apple orchards. Some people have credited El Vergel with saving the apple industry of Chile through the introduction and free distribution of colonies of this insect.

Of the approximately 150 families which supply one or more employees to the farm, 60 live on the mission property. They have a community organization that conducts a recreational program in a large hall and gymnasium located on the farm. Included in the activities are an athletic program, movies, first-aid courses, a blood bank, concerts, and an annual farm fair. Two primary schools are operated on the farm for the children of employees. The physical facilities for these schools and the salary of one teacher are supplied by the mission post. Likewise, a clinic, which serves the families of farm employees, is financed by the mission. It is staffed with a Chilean nurse and an assistant.

In addition to the farm and the social, educational, and medical activities, there are two boarding-schools for students in agriculture and home economics. The home economics school has not yet made a great contribution to education in Chile, but it is not without significance. It was started in 1946 and offers a three-year course to Protestant girls from rural areas who have finished four years of primary school. There are usually no more than 15–20 girls enroled each year. The school is under the direction of a North American home economist who is a Methodist missionary. She has two Chilean assistants, and a few courses are taught by the wives of the missionaries. The curriculum is mainly a continuation of primary-school work, but there are also special classes in sewing, cooking, and similar homemaking activities.

The agricultural school for boys is an old and respected institution. It was started in 1921 and has graduated more than 225 students. The only charge for attendance is 1,000 pesos (approximately $6.50 at mid-1953 rates of exchange) per month for board and room. For the three-year course, students are carefully selected and must have had at least six years of training in primary school before they are admitted. They must also be between sixteen and eighteen years of age at the time of entrance, which means that many of them have completed more than the minimum educational requirements for admission. The curriculum of the school, as shown in Table 12, puts the students through twenty-five to thirty hours of classwork, five hours of physical education, and fifteen hours of farmwork each week. The last is usually directed by the farm foremen, but it is planned by the school faculty so that every boy gets considerable experience in each of the various departments of the farm.

The director of the school is a North American, who also serves as pastor of a near-by Methodist church. He does relatively little teaching, but he has a staff of three full-time and three part-time Chilean teachers and eight missionaries, who teach one or more courses during the school year. The graduates of the school are recognized as well-trained agricultural *técnicos*. Many of them have field positions with various government agencies in Chile—positions which are more or less comparable to those of county ag-

TABLE 12

CURRICULUM OF EL VERGEL'S AGRICULTURAL SCHOOL

Subjects	Hours per Week	Subjects	Hours per Week
First year:		Forestry I...............	5
Arithmetic...............	5	Agricultural plants........	5
Spanish.................	3	Farm buildings...........	5†
Religion...............	5	Practical work on the farm..	15
Zoölogy and botany.......	5	Physical education........	5
General agriculture........	4*	*Third year:*	
Poultry and bee culture....	4†	Spanish.................	3
Horticulture............	2	Mathematics and accounting	3
Biology and hygiene.......	4†	Religion................	4
Gardening...............	4†	Civic education..........	2
Ornithology and entomology	1	Forestry II..............	3
Practical work on the farm..	15	Genetics................	3†
Physical education........	5	Animal husbandry........	5*
Second year:		Veterinary science........	5†
Arithmetic...............	3	Farm management........	3
Spanish.................	4	Agricultural machinery.....	3
Religion................	4	Farm buildings...........	2*
History and geography.....	2	Practical work on the farm..	15
Physics and chemistry.....	5	Physical education........	5

* Two terms only.
† One term only.

ricultural agents in the United States. Some of them have continued their training by attending a university and receiving the degree of *Ingeniero agrónomo,* which is more or less comparable to the Bachelor's degree from a college of agriculture in the United States. Several of the latter group have been employed by the Institute of Inter-American Affairs in its technical assistance program in Chile. They are commonly rated among the best agricultural technicians in Chile, largely because they are willing to "work with their hands" and because they have a good grasp of the practical, as well as the theoretical, problems of agriculture.

During the many years of El Vergel's experience, countless agricultural practices have been tried and proved successful or found wanting. Much experimental work has been done, for example, in finding the best combination of grasses, grazing, and fertilization for good pastures on the hill land of the farm. Likewise, numerous species of trees have been used for reforestation work, and their responses to different soil and climatic situations have been carefully noted. New varieties of fruits and ornamental plants have been developed in the nursery. Much valuable experience has been gained in "top-grafting" different apple stocks with other varieties to obtain heavy-bearing, disease-resistant trees. In connection with the livestock enterprises, attention has been given to the production of low-cost, balanced rations. There is a veritable "gold mine" of agricultural information available at El Vergel.

Although there is surely no other mission in all of Latin America with such a storehouse of tested agricultural information, El Vergel, strangely enough, carries on no agricultural extension service. The same sponsoring agency has a small agricultural extension program near Temuco, about 100 miles south of the El Vergel station, but its program is concerned mainly with the problems of small wheat farmers, who can benefit little by what has been learned at El Vergel in the orchards, pastures, forests, and barns. Here, however, is a body of information that could be of great value to many farmers if it could be communicated to them in ways which they could understand and apply to their own operations.

To develop means by which this accumulated knowledge can be shared with surrounding farmers appears to be a needed next step for this mission station. The great success of El Vergel is largely the result of the work of its director, a man of outstanding ability and vision, who has been in charge of the post since the farm was purchased in 1919. Much of what has been learned is known only to him. If this knowledge is to be preserved and passed along to farmers in Chile, it is important that an extension program get under way before he retires. Indeed, if he were to write a detailed history of the many production practices which he has tried and the lessons that he has learned in his long career as manager of the farm, the result might well be a major contribution to Chilean agriculture.

The farm and accompanying activities at El Vergel obviously comprise an exceptional mission station. The emphasis has been on using the income earned from a large and highly efficient farming operation to support practical educational institutions for young people—institutions that are providing the type of instruction that is badly needed in all of Latin America. At the same time, considerable attention has been given to developing health and social facilities for the numerous farm employees. The record is an enviable one. Except for the lack of a means of transmission of the knowledge gained on the mission farm, there is little about El Vergel that warrants criticism. Moreover, it is highly probable that this station shows the general type of program that would be developed in connection with many of the rural mission posts if only the farms on which they are located were money-making enterprises.

It may be worthwhile to point out that the main secret of success at El Vergel—a farm which represented a heavy investment of mission funds—was in the original purchase of a good land and the appointment of an exceptionally able manager, who has stayed on the job for many years. There have been other favorable factors. Chile has prospered during the period of El Vergel's history and has provided a favorable economic, social, and political environment. Moreover, the climate of Central Chile is similar enough to that found in parts of the United States so that a farm manager trained in the States is not constantly "shooting in the dark" in deciding on his production practices.[6] Even so, religious agencies would do well to learn that there are no substitutes for good land and good farmers if they expect to have self-supporting rural mission stations.

Whereas most of the activities at El Vergel revolve around a farm and have been possible mainly because the farm was profitable, farming is not significant in the following case.

CENTRO RURAL DE CAMOHMILA (TEPOZTLAN, MEXICO)

The Camohmila Rural Center, located about 60 miles from Mexico City, is sponsored by the YMCA of Mexico City and the International Committee of the YMCA. It began as a camp for members of the Mexico City YMCA in 1938. Shortly afterward, the members became interested in helping the small farmers of the surrounding area and employed a doctor to attend to the health needs of the people in Tepoztlan and near-by villages. Later, through the co-operation of the international committee, the rural center was established; a full-time director was employed to develop a program of social reconstruction and rural improvement among the iso-

6. Angol, Chile, is approximately the same distance south of the Equator that San Francisco is north of it.

lated, poverty-stricken villagers and farmers of the area. A comprehensive program has been in operation for approximately a decade.

The present director, who was hired in 1948, was reared on a farm in Mississippi and is an agricultural-college graduate with experience in both rural YMCA work and extension service activities in the United States. His predecessor was an agricultural missionary with many years of experience in India before he came to Mexico. Throughout its history the center has never had more than one North American couple on its regular staff. The salaries of the two North Americans have been paid by the international committee. All other expenditures have come from the Mexico City chapter of the YMCA and a few other local donors, including recent, unexpended grants of about $30,000 from Sears, Roebuck and Company of Mexico.

All activities except the recreational camp assist rural families to raise their level of living. There are approximately ten mountain villages reached with one or more services from the Rural Center. The center itself is located on about 15 acres of valley land on the edge of Tepoztlan. The emphasis of the program is on training rural people to provide a better living for themselves, but there are several important activities which go considerably beyond the field of training.

Community health program.—One of the vital aspects of the center's program is the health work, which is directed by a trained Mexican nurse, who has a small clinic and emergency room in one of the headquarters buildings. She also travels by car, by horse, or on foot to bring medicines and nursing care to isolated rural homes. One of her regular projects is the inoculation of school children in the surrounding villages and the maintenance of first-aid kits in the village schools. She usually presides over 150–200 births per year, only a few of which are in the clinic. She gives prenatal care to all women who come to the center and treats hundreds of patients each year, both in their homes and at the clinic, for various illnesses and accidents.

Nursery school.—A day nursery, started in 1952, now cares for fifteen to twenty-five preschool children at a time. The children receive a balanced meal each day at lunch time; moreover, they are examined regularly by the nurse, who inoculates them against common diseases. They are weighed every three months, and careful records are kept of their growth and general physical condition. Although many of them are so malnourished at the time they enter the nursery school that they have little energy for ordinary children's games, after two or three months of improved food and good nursing care, most become healthy, vigorous youngsters.

Scholarships.—The center regularly offers ten to twelve scholarships to boys from neighboring mountain villages where there are no schools. The boys live in a small domitory at the center and attend regular classes in the Tepoztlan public school. They spend one to two hours a day working at agricultural and construction tasks at the center and are provided with clothes and school supplies, as well as room and board and 1 peso a week for spending money. The nurse takes her meals with the boys and teaches them table manners. The students, usually twelve to sixteen years of age, start in the second grade. If they do well in their school work, they stay at Camohmila until they have completed the sixth grade. A few have gone on to high school on their own initiative. In addition, a few girls have been aided by scholarships and placed in boarding-schools in Mexico City. One girl helped by the scholarship program graduated with the highest rating in her class in 1952 and subsequently entered a normal school.

Recreational camp.—The camp, which occupies roughly one-third of the land area of Camohmila, is an important source of income and one of the few organized camps in the country. Its facilities include a few cottages, two dormitory buildings, a large kitchen and dining hall, a swimming pool, and playing fields for football, basketball, and volleyball, as well as equipment for table tennis, croquet, horseshoe-pitching, and similar sports. It is used primarily by groups from Mexico City, such as the YMCA, Boy Scouts, Girl Scouts, Sunday-school classes, organizations of government workers, employees' clubs, and occasionally by North American tourists who want to get a taste of life in rural Mexico. Many of the groups which use it come out for one day of picnicking, but others stay for several days at a time.

The camp rates depend on the nature of the group, the type of food served, and the amount of service expected. The income from the camp largely finances the program of community services. Within recent years the construction of excellent roads between Tepoztlan and Mexico City and Cuernavaca has greatly expanded the potentialities of the camp as an incomer-earner.

Weaving enterprise.—One of the buildings at the center is, in effect, a small factory in which teen-age girls from the near-by villages learn the art of weaving. They work seven and one-half hours a day and are paid on a piecework basis. On hand looms the cotton, rayon, and nylon yarns purchased by the center are woven into tablecloths, napkins, bedspreads, hand towels, and small rugs, to be sold to retail stores in Mexico City.

When the weaving department was started, the women and girls were expected to follow the trade in their homes after a training period at the center. Experience proved, however, that few housewives are interested in learning to weave and that most of the girls would rather come to work than take a loom to their homes. Consequently, weaving has developed into an important commercial enterprise, employing 15–25 girls under the tutelage of a skilled native weaver. Their daily earnings average about the same as wages paid a man for full-time farmwork in the community. In 1952 the gross income of the weaving project was approximately 50,000 pesos (equivalent to about $6,000). There are always many more girls requesting training and employment in the weaving department than can be accepted. Not only are the net receipts from the weaving enterprise important to the center, but the earnings of the girls are appreciable additions to their families' incomes.

Agricultural extension service.—The extension activities of Camohmila radiate from headquarters to school children and adults in the surrounding countryside. For example, one of the long-standing needs of local farmers has been met by the director without placing a financial burden on the center. He is importing day-old chicks from the United States by airplane, keeping them at the center until they are about one month old, and then vaccinating them and selling them to farmers. Although some of the farmers are beginning to keep small breeding flocks, most of the birds purchased from the center are sold in near-by public markets as fryers or roasters. For this reason, the farmers prefer a meat-type chicken.

The first efforts to improve poultry in the villages served by the center were to sell hatching eggs from the breeding flocks of New Hampshire Reds and Plymouth Rocks kept at the center and to exchange surplus roosters with the farmers for their game cocks. Although these features of the poultry improvement program are still continued, experience has shown that the importation of baby chicks from the United States, brooding them until they are at least a month old, and selling or trading them to farmers constitute a much more efficient way of increasing poultry production in the area. In 1952, over 6,000 chicks were placed with farmers, and in 1953 the number was almost doubled.

The center also keeps three to five purebred sows, from which pigs are produced for distribution within the community. Purebred pigs are sold directly to farmers or traded for their scrub stock. A group program has also been started in which a club of farm boys is given a purebred gilt. The club repays the center out of the first litter by returning a gilt, which will then be given to another club. The center also keeps one or two boars to which farmers may breed their sows free of charge.

Both the poultry and hog enterprises are usually operated without loss to the center; however, no attempt is made to realize more than a very small profit from them.

A large irrigated garden not only supplies part of the food for the recreational camp but also produces vegetables which are sold in Mexico City. At the same time, it serves as a demonstration of good gardening practices and has been a means of introducing several new vegetables into the area. There is also a bee-keeping enterprise at the center, with modern hives and a honey extractor. The equipment is loaned to private bee-keepers, who may buy basic supplies at cost. The center bottles its honey and sells it in Mexico City; it will do the same for local bee-keepers if they wish to avail themselves of this marketing service. It was originally hoped that the canning of local fruits for sale in urban centers would provide employment for several women as a profitable local industry. As yet, however, the canning enterprise has been insignificant because of the high cost of equipment, the lack of experience on the part of local women, and the small volume of fruit suitable for canning.

In addition to the enterprises described previously, within the last two years the center has carried on a series of fertilizer and variety demonstrations with garden and field crops. An important educational program resembling that of a county agricultural agent in the United States has also been developed. It is carried out by a Mexican, who was hired when the director, though a successful extension agent in the United States, was unable to influence the native farmers. The Mexican extension worker was reared on a farm and trained practically in agriculture, but he is not a graduate of an accredited college of agriculture. Nevertheless, he was able, within one year, to establish a good foundation for an educational program among farm families in the neighboring rural villages. He has organized clubs in schools and village committees of farmers as the principal mechanisms for his teaching of improved farm and home practices. Like county agents in this country, he makes visits and gives demonstrations to small groups of farmers.

Camohmila is obviously similar to many other agricultural mission stations. In its health work, its nursery school and scholarship program, and its agricultural projects, it shares many of the characteristics of mission posts described earlier. There are some points of difference, however, that are worth noting.

For instance, it relies on the recreational camp and the weaving enterprise as its profit-making activities. Mission stations of this type usually try to make money from farming, to support a program of community services. Farming usually requires a heavy investment, too often results in a loss instead of a profit, and thus acts as a financial brake on the scope of other activities. By importing baby chicks, raising a few good pigs, and maintaining a large garden, the center sustains only "break-even" agricultural enterprises. The success of its other ventures depends on the proximity of a large city, an urban-rural relationship of the sort that could be turned to profit by many missions. Moreover, enterprises of this character need not be limited to weaving; there are other activities, such as pottery-making and woodworking, suitable to the skills and needs of rural people.

Two aspects of the agricultural extension program at Camohmila may be significant for community developers throughout Latin America. First, the local operating unit involves more activities than those ordinarily engaged in by an extension service in the United States. For example, Camohmila's animals are a source of breeding stock; its gardens and demonstration plots provide seeds and plants for distribution; it markets honey for neighboring farmers and could probably expand its marketing service to other products. In short, the extension office in an isolated area may have to take on some of the supply and marketing functions that are ordinarily accomplished by business firms in more highly developed areas. It is notable that one of these functions—the importation of chicks—has been a first-rate technique for improving agriculture. Second, the staff at the center has learned that the direct educational phases of the extension program—the advisory work with farmers and school children —was not very successful until a native worker was employed. This should be of interest to all agencies operating rural development programs in Latin America.

The subsidy provided by the YMCA of Mexico City and the international committee is usually less than $2,500 per year. An interesting question is whether a mission post of this type could be completely self-supporting. Could one North American couple with the small capital investment represented by the physical plant at Camohmila—about $15,000–$20,000—develop a combination of profit-making, educational, and community service activities that would eliminate the necessity for annual donations from outside sources? Actual experience at the center does not provide a positive answer to this question. Much, of course, would depend on how much health and educational work is done relative to the time and resources devoted to the income-producing activities. Camohmila, however, has for several years been close enough to the "break-even" point to suggest that it might rather easily become self-supporting and still render a very significant service to rural families.

As a final example of agricultural mission work, we turn to the case of a unique college of agriculture in Brazil. It is apparently the only mission-sponsored school in Latin America which offers university-level training in agriculture.

ESCOLA SUPERIOR DE AGRICULTURA DE LAVRAS, INSTITUTO GAMMON (LAVRAS, BRAZIL)

The Lavras Agricultural College is an old, well-known, and highly respected mission project in Latin America. It is one of several schools which make up Gammon Institute, a virtually self-supporting institution owned by the Board of World Missions of the Presbyterian Church in the United States, which also pays a part of the salaries of the missionaries who constitute the governing board and directing staff. The institute was founded as a small mission school at Campinas in the state of São Paulo in 1869. Because of a serious epidemic of yellow fever in that area, it was moved to Lavras in the state of Minas Gerais in 1893.

The School of Agriculture was founded in 1908, well in advance of the time when most religious agencies had become seriously interested in sending agricultural missionaries to Latin America. Moreover, there was little interest among Brazilians at that time in the teaching of scientific agriculture. Throughout its history, it has been "close to the soil." Its directors have not only recognized the need for improving rural life in Brazil but have raised an institution whose graduates have made worthwhile contributions to rural welfare.

The school has two curriculums. One is a four-year course at the university level for students who have completed twelve years of primary and secondary schooling. Graduates of this course receive the degree of *Ingeniero agrónomo*. The other curriculum provides a three-year practical course in agriculture for students who have finished nine years of primary and junior high school work. The graduates are called *técnicos*. They cannot enter a university to study for the degree of *Ingeniero agrónomo* unless and until they finish the last three years of the regular high-school curriculum. The three-year practical course is similar to that of several mission-sponsored schools in Latin America. The four-year university course, on the other hand, is unique among agricultural activities sponsored by religious agencies in Latin America.

From the inception of the school through 1952, there had been 354 graduates, of whom 268 had finished the requirements for the degree of *Ingeniero agrónomo*. In recent years, there were usually about 75 students enrolled, less than one-third of whom are taking the three-year practical course. All thirteen faculty members, except the director of the school and an assistant who is in charge of the practical course, are Brazilians. The two North Americans are graduates of good colleges of agriculture in the United States. The director has a Master's degree in agriculture, has done considerable graduate work in the United States, and has had many years of experience at Lavras. He is recognized as one of the top-ranking agricultural missionaries in Latin America.

The requirements for the four-year course are similar to those of land-grant colleges in the United States. The Lavras school is relatively small and not highly departmentalized; hence there are no provisions for third- and four-year students to major specifically in such subjects as agronomy, agricultural engineering, animal husbandry, or horticulture, as is commonly the case in the United States. However, the requirements include a strong central core of science courses—botany, zoölogy, chemistry, mathematics, and physics—plus the usual work in soils, crops, farm buildings, animal nutrition, veterinary medicine, and similar applied subjects. All students are required to work on the college farm as a part of their regular training during their Freshman and Sophomore years.

The school operates a 300-acre farm, but it does very little experimental work. The farm customarily loses money, and neither the production practices, organization of enterprises, nor condition of the fields are noticeably better than those on good plantations in the area. Nevertheless, the school has made such a place for itself in Brazilian agricultural circles that it now receives an annual subsidy of 300,000 cruzieros (equivalent in 1953 to about $7,500) from the federal government and an equal amount from the state government. Many of its graduates occupy important positions in state and federal agricultural programs.

Why is it that the Lavras College of Agriculture has been able to attain the enviable position which it now enjoys in Brazil? Many factors are no doubt important, but there are at least three of paramount significance.

First, the college was started before much had been done by Brazilian governmental agencies, either federal or state, in the way of assisting agriculture. It was the first college of agriculture in Minas Gerais. It was one of the early institutions in Brazil to lift an agricultural curriculum to the university level of study. By giving scientific agriculture the status of a professional career, it attracted the sons of wealthy farmers. They no longer had to become lawyers, physicians, or politicians to maintain social status; agriculture no longer put a man in the class of a farm foreman or an estate manager.

Second, the founder was a dynamic person who had much more than an academic interest in agricultural problems. He organized and guided an annual agricultural fair, at which farmers in the surrounding area exhibited their products. He organized a swine-breeders' association, imported purebred Duroc Jersey hogs from the United States, and carried on an educational campaign to increase hog production. Lavras became a center of enthusiasm for modernizing agriculture and a fountainhead of information. Thousands of copies of extension bulletins and circulars have been distributed by the college. Four of the first five national corn shows in Brazil were organized by the director. In short, the school was a live and throbbing agricultural center which served the farmers of the area with a new type of knowledge about a new kind of agriculture.

Third, the early graduates of Lavras became famous because they possessed a spirit of service and a willingness to indulge in the practical. The college taught them how to work with their hands and how to think their way through practical problems. It was largely because of this Lavras influence that Minas Gerais hired a North American to organize its School of Agriculture in the Rural University at Viçosa, and to develop it into an institution that would instill practical knowledge and a spirit of service into its graduates. Moreover, after the period of organization was over, a subsequent director of the School of Agriculture at Viçosa was a United States citizen who had spent several years as an agricultural missionary in China. It is rare that missionary effort can show such a direct and important influence on Latin-American institutions.

Today, the two schools—one mission-sponsored and the other state-supported—are the sources of some of the best trained *Ingenieros agrónomos* in Latin America. Both institutions have been greatly influenced by North American methods, values, and ideas. Both are making worthwhile contributions to Brazilian agriculture. In recent years, however, the publicly supported Rural University is forging far ahead of the mission-supported school at Lavras. It is to the credit of the missionary enterprise that the latter led the way, but it has not had the resources to maintain its trailblazing position. Indeed, it is doubtful, now that government support of agricultural colleges is an accepted idea, that any unendowed private institution can maintain a position of leadership in the training of agricultural students. This is the problem facing Lavras. Its early work was outstanding; its future is not clear.

5 CONCLUSIONS AND RECOMMENDATIONS

The preceding chapters have been concerned with two main topics: first, a brief description of some of the principal characteristics of Latin-American culture and, second, an exposition of the scope and nature of the technical assistance work of United States religious agencies in Latin America. In these chapters many judgments have been expressed, and recommendations have been made about ways and means by which the missionary effort might be improved. Most of these, however, have concerned individual mission projects or particular types of problems with which the religious agencies have been wrestling. This report would hardly be complete without comments of this nature, but they are not adequate for a view of the whole.

The aim of the present chapter is to place the technical features of the total missionary effort in a frame of reference which permits conclusions about their relevancy and adequacy. To do this, one must understand the objectives of the missionary enterprise, and one must view the means used to achieve them in relation to the major characteristics of the Latin-American culture.

In an ultimate sense all missionary activity is aimed at achieving man's spiritual salvation. There are, however, more immediate objectives, toward the realization of which the missionaries are often working. In general, these aims are of two types: one group of goals is concerned with the implementing of ideas and mechanisms that spread "the Gospel message"; the other group is concerned with improving man's welfare on earth.

Missionary activity which is aimed primarily at achieving the first type of goal is likely to attempt direct methods and techniques that influence large numbers of people to accept Christianity and that encourage them to establish and support church organizations and to erect, maintain, and decorate buildings for purposes of worship. On the other hand, missionary activity which is concerned primarily with the second type of goal—the improvement of man's

100

welfare on earth—is likely to try organizing and operating schools, hospitals, agricultural projects, and similar activities that tend to improve the state of the arts and the level of living of the people.

A large number of religious organizations do not engage in this latter type of activity. More than 175 United States religious agencies send missionaries to Latin America, but only 65–70 of them sponsor technical assistance projects. Most of the organizations which refuse to engage in this type of work do not reject the desirability of improving man's welfare, but they insist that this can be done most effectively by "cleansing his soul" or that it is not a proper function for a religious agency.

On the other hand, there are some religious organizations that do not engage in missionary activity except when it is related in some manner to technical activities. Among these denominations, such projects are usually viewed as manifesting religious values, in and of themselves, because they meet genuine human needs which God's love of man would like to have fulfilled. Missionaries of these agencies believe that in helping their fellow-man to meet his needs of education, health, and physical sustenance they are carrying forward God's desire and are thus identifying themselves with his aspirations.

Other agencies appear to hold a middle-of-the-road position with respect to these technical projects. They view the schools, hospitals, agricultural activities, and similar projects as necessary intermediate steps in the fight to win men's souls to God or, in particular cases, to increase the membership of the church of the sponsoring denomination. Each project is appraised, in part, in terms of its ability to bring men closer to God in a formal religious manner.

Even among those denominations which emphasize the direct and immediate spiritual values of the technical assistance projects, there is rarely complete reliance on them as the sole instruments for reaching the religious objective. For instance, missionaries who are engaged primarily in secular activities, such as treating patients in a hospital or teaching farmers how to improve their production practices, are also expected, as a minimum, to exemplify good Christian lives. Sometimes they are expected to engage part time in some type of activity which is explicitly aimed at teaching people to understand Christian doctrines or denominational dogma.

Notwithstanding the direct religious implications attributed, in varying degree by different denominations, to technical activities, this report has been quite purposely limited to a consideration of such projects as means of attaining the welfare goal. The central question is: How adequate and how effective have these technical service activities been in improving the well-being of the people of Latin America? There are three pertinent aspects to this question, each of which will be discussed. They are (1) the efficiency with which the religious agencies have used their resources; (2) the professional quality of their work; and (3) the adequacy of the missionary organization for performing the tasks that are needed.

The Efficiency Problem

The technical activities of the religious agencies have been centered mainly on education, health, and agriculture. Have they been wise in putting primary attention on these three fields of activity? In doing so, have they used their resources efficiently? In general, the answer to these questions is "yes." Latin-American culture has placed a low premium on the education, health, and nutrition of the masses. Partly as a consequence of this, the productivity of the region's economy has been hampered, and the impact of non-democratic forces in its society has been strengthened. The religious agencies, therefore, in pursuit of their welfare goal, not only have gone directly to the center of their concern, namely, the people, but they have done this in areas of activity in which the existing culture needs the assistance and the competition of outside forces. Education, health, and agriculture have been the centers of attention of both public and private technical assistance agencies in Latin America. Historically, the religious agencies led the way.

That they were generally on sound ground in tackling these three problems does not mean, however, that they might not also wisely have given emphasis to others. For example, it is entirely probable that assistance to isolated villagers in constructing farm-to-market roads would, in many instances, have been a more productive use of resources than the establishment of some of the agricultural projects. The development of small factories or cottage industries to manufacture consumer goods appears suitable for missionary projects in some areas. Likewise, the promotion of recreational programs and facilities, both as a source of income to a mission station (such as the recreational camp at the Camohmila Rural Center of the YMCA at Tepoztlan, Mexico) and as activities for raising the level of living of underprivileged people, probably has more potentialities than most religious agencies recognize. These are but examples of some of the types of projects which the missionary enterprise might have sponsored and which appear to be as relevant and fruitful, under many conditions, as those on which most emphasis has been centered.

No doubt, there are other kinds of projects which would be equally appropriate for the many different environmental situations found in Latin America. It would be particularly unfortunate if the missionary agencies should fall into a stereotype of promoting schools, hospitals, and agricultural projects as the only constructive outlets for their technical assistance work. Moreover, conditions in Latin America have changed significantly since the original patterns of missionary activity were established, and the traditional types of projects may be considerably less appropriate in the future than they have been in the past.

It is not sufficient merely to indicate that the general fields of education, health, and agriculture have been soundly chosen. A further question worthy of consideration is the following: Have the particular activities which have been emphasized within each of the three fields yielded the greatest returns relative to the effort expended? Numerous comments have been made in the preceding chapter in regard to this question.

About education, for instance, repeated reference has been made to the fact that many of the large, well-financed schools sponsored by the agencies are devoting most of their resources to teaching a traditional type of curriculum very similar to that taught by the regular public schools in Latin America, whereas there is great need in many countries for new types of schools and a reorientation of curriculums and teaching methods in the existing institutions. The principal impediments to commonly needed changes have been pointed out.[1] They are serious. A shift in emphasis in the educational work of the agencies merits much consideration.

1. Cf. particularly pp. 40; 49–51.

The nature of the problem is in part exemplified by the remarks of an executive secretary of a foreign mission board of one of the large denominations. "Thirty or forty years ago," he said, "we were leading the way in the establishment of school standards and curriculums. Today, we are kept busy complying with government regulations." In other words, Latin-American governments have stepped into the educational field and have crystallized into laws and regulations many ideas that the early missionaries were sponsoring. Most of the missionary schools are therefore no longer in the forefront of educational developments. They are conforming to existing practices and procedures. Within the prevailing framework they usually maintain high standards, and the examples which they set and the competition which they give are worth while. To recapture positions of leadership, however, they must branch off from the traditional and develop new types of schools and new courses in their existing schools.

In particular, it appears that the religious agencies have not made the most of their opportunity to establish schools that constructively serve the children of lower-class families. There are many primary schools sponsored by missionaries which are available to the children of small farmers and urban workers. However, they are commonly limited to the traditional reading, writing, and arithmetic through the first four or five grades. These institutions are certainly not without merit, but there is a tremendous need for the teaching of vocational skills and for citizenship training in nearly all Latin-American countries.

There are many different ways in which this problem might be attacked. Among them, the following suggestions should receive consideration:

1. The well-established primary and secondary schools of the religious agencies, which are usually in cities of fairly large size, could offer more courses in technical fields, including vocational skills and methods of teaching. In some countries such courses might have to be in addition to, and outside of, the regular curriculum required by the ministry of education. Some of them could be offered in evening classes for students who work during the day.

2. Some of the large primary and secondary institutions could probably

organize special technical and commercial schools, in connection with their present facilities, which would provide specialized training for students who are not interested in the regular secondary course of study. This is the pattern followed by Mackenzie Institute in São Paulo, Brazil, in the establishment of its commercial and technical schools.[2] In most such cases these specialized schools should probably be open only to those students who have finished four to six years of primary study. Their curriculums, of course, would include some of the same subjects that are taught in the regular secondary course, but emphasis would be on preparing students to work in their chosen trade or profession after a total of ten to twelve years of schooling, instead of preparing them for the university.

3. There is very great need for a large number of primary schools that teach skills in various types of trades and in agriculture to serve the children of poor families who will probably never get more than three or four years of schooling. A large proportion of the children in Latin America have never set foot in a schoolroom, and a majority probably never go to school for more than four years. This means that there are large numbers of unmarried, partially employed children from twelve to eighteen years of age in practically every village and rural area who will not be reached by simply increasing the number of primary schools which limit their courses to the traditional reading, writing, and arithmetic. The significance of such institutions as Colegio San José, Bluefields, Nicaragua; Instituto Rural Evangélico, Itapina, Brazil; and the ORT Vocational Center, Rio de Janeiro, Brazil, lies in the fact that they are combining vocational work with most of the essentials of regular primary schooling.[3] Not only does this approach have an appeal to children who may be "teen-agers" still in the primary grades, but it also recognizes the great need for skilled workers in Latin America. Finally, it offers constructive training to the kind of student who will rarely go to school more than four or five years during his entire life.

In all attempts on the part of United States religious agencies to approach the educational problems of Latin America anew, a definite effort to "upgrade" the prestige value of "working with one's hands" is in order. Many of the existing missionary schools are geared to prevailing value-judgments, which tend to equate social status to a type of white-collar employment in which "the educated

2. See pp. 52–55.   3. See pp. 55–63.

man" disdains physical labor. This has come about largely because these schools have fallen into outworn patterns that do not develop skilled artisans and highly productive farmers.

In the field of health the hospitals, the clinics, and the few nursing schools sponsored by United States religious agencies have made worthwhile contributions in treating patients and training nurses. Even more important, perhaps, is the influence of the medical missionaries in turning the attention of governments to the medical needs of the poorer classes. In an increasing number of countries, however, governments are now providing medical facilities of the same type as those sponsored by the religious agencies. The needs for such facilities are so tremendous that the combined efforts of the government and the religious agencies are far from sufficient. There is, therefore, a sound basis for continuing the mission institutions. At the same time, it should be recognized that few of the medical missionaries are pioneering new methods and techniques. They are practicing about the same kind of medicine as the better-trained national doctors, but with a little more emphasis on reaching poor people.

In practically all countries the major work of the medical missionaries is in curative medicine, whereas the great challenge is in the field of preventive medicine. A given amount of money spent to teach large numbers of people a few simple practices about good nutrition, personal hygiene, and home sanitation would almost assuredly do more to improve health conditions than if it were spent to equip and operate hospitals and clinics. Moreover, the techniques and methods of preventive medicine are much less well developed in Latin America than are those of curative medicine. There is both a challenge and an opportunity in this situation.

In regard to agriculture, the following excerpts from a statement writen by Dr. J. B. Griffing[4] about rural mission posts in both Asia and Latin America give an excellent summary applicable to the Latin-American situation:

4. Dr. Griffing was for several years an agricultural missionary in China. Later he had extensive experience in Latin America: as director of the School of Agriculture in the Rural University of Minas Gerais at Viçosa, Brazil; as a directing technician with the Institute of Inter-American Affairs during World War II; and as director of the program of the American International Association in Brazil. Throughout his life he has been a participant in, or a student of, rural mission activities.

Agricultural Colleges

. . . At the time these were established, they were pioneers in a field where the training of able agricultural leaders was badly needed. The graduates they have turned out have rendered a splendid service, but, in general, the period when the agricultural mission filled a vacuum on this level has passed. Many countries which a generation ago had no agricultural colleges now actually have too many competing institutions on the higher level.

The fact must be kept in mind that the cost of establishing a degree-granting agricultural school is many times greater than that of an academic college, and the disparity in costs is increasing rapidly.

Agricultural Schools or Institutes of Secondary or Primary Grade

There are, of course, many more of these than of the colleges, and it is possible for them to link more closely to the rural areas that they serve. There is, however, a common fallacy on the part of workers both from the United States and of the people served. This belief is that if an institution has a tract of land, it may, through student labor, become self-supporting. Such an assumption is far from the truth and often leads to disaster. An agricultural school must have (*a*) a substantial budget; (*b*) personnel trained in practical agriculture; and (*c*) a director or manager with outstanding business ability. With such assets there are circumstances where an agricultural school may meet a real need.

Agricultural Experimentation

Many missionaries have made notable contributions through the introduction of better plants, animals, and techniques. The operation of an experiment station, however, could hardly be considered a function of agricultural missions. At the present time, experimentation is so highly developed and widespread on the part of both native scientists and those from technical agencies abroad that there is little need for the church to compete in a field where great expense and much time are involved.

It is rather the function of the agricultural missions to make use of the findings that these scientists have turned out and carry them to their own constituencies through a system of popularization and extension.

Demonstration Farm

In general, the same principle holds for the demonstration farm as for the experiment station.

Food-Supply Farm

One of the most common of all agricultural projects in the mission field is the farm upon which food is grown for a boarding-school or some humanitarian institution. One rather surprising fact about such farms is that very few of them pay expenses. Lack of practical agricultural experience in the country being served, inadequacy of student labor, and lack of good business management are the chief causes of the difficulty. With many institutions where the farm had no educational function, food might be produced more economically on a contract basis under supervision than by direct operation. It would seem futile for a mission to export agricultural personnel to perform a task which a local truck gardener could provide at a much lower cost.

Community Leadership

Agricultural missions may find some of their best opportunities for service through community leadership. This may include agricultural extension; the organization of co-operatives; technical aid in community production and marketing of products; health services; clubs for women; 4H-type clubs for boys and girls; exhibits, fairs, and educational meetings; recreational activities, such as games, sports, and singing.

The community leadership may be part of the program of an agricultural school or it may be a service of the rural church where there is no agricultural school. Every mission agricultural school certainly should maintain a program of community service as a laboratory in which students could be trained.

One of the advantages of the community service program is that a few capable leaders can carry the impact of agricultural missions to many people throughout a wide area at comparatively low expense . . . there are many new techniques in agricultural improvement or rural betterment which may be passed on to the rural people through rural pastors and workers of the national church. . . .

The community program is subject to the highest degree of adaptation to local conditions. It is one where educational materials, printed, visual, or demonstration, may be given a wide range of use. It is a type of approach which may accomplish much for little and in a comparatively short time. . . . It offers the greatest opportunity for agricultural missions today.

To recapitulate what has been said in regard to the types of projects emphasized by the religious agencies, the main points are as follows:

1. The agencies have been on sound ground in emphasizing the three fields of education, health, and agriculture, but there are others which also offer worthwhile opportunities.

2. Within each of the fields, there are significant areas which offer potentialities for constructive and efficient work as good as, or better than, some of those that are receiving major attention.

3. The increased emphasis which governments are giving to the educational, health, and agricultural needs of the people has limited the pace-setting, or pioneering, nature of many mission activities. There is, therefore, a real need for the religious agencies critically to review their programs, with a view to bringing them up to date to meet conditions that have changed significantly since original patterns were established.

It must always be remembered, however, in suggesting changes in emphasis that even the combined effort of all the public and private agencies in the fields of education, health, and agriculture still falls far short of meeting real and important needs of the expanding population of Latin America. The task, therefore, is not one of reducing the volume of the technical work of United States religious agencies but of remolding it so that there can be greater accomplishments with the resources available.

Quality and Performance

The immediately preceding discussion has pertained to the emphasis being given to different types of missionary activity. The center of concern has been the problem of efficiency—the results achieved in relation to the effort expended. This has included the possibility of achieving greater results by alternative uses of available resources. This is an important aspect of the total problem.

There is, however, the additional question of how well the missionaries are doing their work in the activities on which they are engaged. To ask how wisely the religious agencies have utilized their resources of manpower and funds by emphasizing education, health, agriculture, and certain areas of activity within each of these fields is quite different from asking how well the missionaries assigned to these activities have performed their work. A doctor, for instance, might be more fruitfully employed in teaching people the elements of personal hygiene and home sanitation than in treating patients who come to a hospital; but there is still the question of how competently he does the latter. This is a question to be judged in terms of professional standards and of performance related to these standards. In earlier sections of this report, particularly chapter 4, many comments have already been made on this general topic. The following, therefore, mainly summarizes what has already been said or implied.

Lay opinions with respect to the professional competence of medical missionaries may be of dubious value. Nevertheless, it is highly probable that a larger proportion of the medical missionaries are better trained, hence professionally more competent, than those engaged in educational or agricultural work. This results mainly from the specific and relatively high standards that have to be met before doctors and nurses can obtain licenses to practice. There are other indications that lead the layman to the conclusion that the medical missionaries maintain high standards of performance. For instance, it is quite common for the top-ranking members of the local medical profession to practice in mission-sponsored hospitals. North Americans, both in business and in government positions, who live in cities which have hospitals sponsored by the agencies, usually testify to the high professional standards of such institutions. This is commonly true even among members of this group who depend on national doctors for their medical care. There is nearly always praise for the nursing care received at such hospitals. Finally, the appearance of the buildings, the cleanliness of the rooms, the hours of work, the punctuality of the staffs, and the orderliness with which the crowds of clinic patients are handled, all indicate that the large medical institutions of the religious agencies are well managed and efficient.

There are, of course, a great number of small clinics or treatment-rooms, in connection with schools and rural mission posts which are not staffed by professional personnel from the United States. Many of these are under the direction of locally trained nurses, some of whom give simple treatments as well as provide nursing care. In connection with such clinics, there is usually a local doctor who can be called for consultation about any case beyond the competence of the nurse. Some of the small, isolated schools have treatment-rooms for students; these are often reported in the statistics of mission activities as "clinics" which are not supervised by either professional nurses or doctors. Usually, a missionary who has had a first-aid course or is otherwise adept at giving injections and dressing small wounds is in charge of these treatment-rooms. Medical care in connection with such situations is rarely anything more than that which thousands of housewives in this country commonly do in treating the cuts, bruises, burns, colds, and sore throats of their children.

Both types of clinic—that is, those under the direction of a trained nurse and those in the charge of a lay person—are often quite important to the health of local residents. No doubt, many highly trained medical people would put a rather low rating on the quality of this type of service. Nevertheless, when it is compared with the quackery, witchcraft, and "patent medicines" which are prevalent in many rural areas of Latin America, it is often superior to any other medical service available locally.

In the educational field the United States missionaries are less important as teachers than as school administrators. Although most of those who are connected with large primary and secondary schools teach one or two courses, their significant influence is in connection with such functions as selecting teachers; determining salary scales and tuition charges; developing curriculums and deciding on the content of courses (to the extent that these things are not done by laws and government regulations); and performing the myriads of detailed administrative duties involved in operating a school. Even in the numerous small primary schools sponsored by religious agencies, the main task of the missionary may be wholly administrative. One man, for instance, may have under his jurisdiction a dozen or more such schools staffed by native teachers. In such cases he usually has evangelistic duties as well, which are quite separate and distinct from his functions as school administrator.

There is great variation in the professional training and experience of the educational missionaries. Many of them were schoolteachers in the United States before they became missionaries. Some have had considerable training in educational methods and child psychology. A few have had college training in school administration, and others have held positions as school principals or superintendents in their own country. However, there are others who had little specialized training or experience in either teaching or school administration before they were assigned to their mission posts. Education is, of course, a field to which the person trained as an evangelist can rather easily turn his attention. There is, therefore, a strong temptation for missionary agencies to expect men who have been trained primarily as pastors or priests in this country to function as teachers and school administrators in their mission assignments.

The rather heterogeneous backgrounds of the educational missionaries notwithstanding, the great majority of the schools sponsored by United States religious agencies rank at least in the upper half of comparable schools in most of the Latin-American countries. A few of them are right at the top of the list, and most are well above average. At practically all levels of instruction the missionary agencies have succeeded in recruiting better-than-average native teachers. They usually provide a physical plant and equipment which is as good as, and sometimes better than, that of other public and private schools of comparable grade in the surrounding area.

In addition, there appears to be a high degree of enthusiasm among the native teachers for the intellectual atmosphere around the mission schools. Many of them in the larger cities teach part time at a mission school and part time at a public school. It is not unusual for one of these teachers to say: "When I come to this school [the mission school] I feel as if I am entering a new world." It is difficult for them to explain the exact nature of the "new world," but it is clear that it is a pleasing experience, which is connected with the interrelationships among fellow faculty members, on the one hand, and among students and teachers, on the other.

In most of the large mission-sponsored schools, there is not only a better-than-average teaching staff working in a better-than-average environment, but, as contrasted with most public schools, there is usually more emphasis on English, on team sports and physical education, on extracurricular activities of various types, and less adherence to the dictation method of teaching. In the small, scattered primary schools, particularly in rural areas, where the influence of the United States missionaries is not of a day-by-day nature, it is difficult to see that the mission-sponsored schools are significantly better than others of the same type. Some have superior teachers, who are sure of receiving their pay on schedule, which is not always the case with public school teachers. Mainly, however, the scattered, rural, primary schools sponsored by the religious agencies are of significance because they usually afford a meager educational opportunity to children who would otherwise not be able to attend any kind of school.

Although the quality of mission-sponsored schools is generally quite high, there is considerable room for improvement. The following criteria are suggested as three means to improve the quality of many schools:

1. More constructive attention should be given to improved teaching methods. There are many legitimate differences of opinion about the *best* way in which to present subject matter to children of different ages. Nevertheless, the common Latin-American method of teaching appears to put far too much stress on memory work. Teachers dictate, and students memorize. The basic theory behind this approach is that there is a given body of knowledge to be passed from generation to generation and that the most efficient way to do this is for the teacher and textbook-writer to organize this knowledge into neat little packages and "pound it into the heads of youngsters" as quickly and expeditiously as possible.

It may be only the extremists who will insist that this whole basic theory is wrong, particularly with respect to developing the elementary skills of reading, writing, and arithmetic. Nevertheless, when this approach is pushed too far, it certainly robs the student of the opportunity to practice thinking for himself, discovering and organizing information in his own way, and reaching judgments about problems which involve winnowing and weighing information and points of view from many different sources.

Because of the deep cultural roots of the prevailing methods of teaching, changes in such methods will be slow and difficult to achieve. The ways and means of improving them should be the work of skilled specialists, not a part-time side line of a busy school administrator or evangelist. The religious agencies would be taking a step in the right direction if they obtained the services of a few such specialists to travel from school to school for the purpose of training the staffs in new approaches to the teaching problem.

2. There is a dearth of good textbooks and teaching materials in most of the Latin-American countries. This is a problem to which the agencies might well give attention. The preparation of Spanish and Portuguese Sunday-school lessons and various types of Christian literature, for use in evangelistic work, has received considerably more attention by most agencies than teaching materials for their schools.

Great progress has been made in the United States during the past quarter-century, in improving the books used in elementary grades. For instance, in kindergarten and in the first five years of grade school, much attention has been given to expanding the child's vocabulary by a sequence of stories, usually amply illustrated with colored pictures, which are carefully designed to introduce a given number of new words and phrases in each story. These are then repeated in subsequent stories sufficiently often that the child learns their meaning without becoming conscious of the problem of definitions. The selection, ordering, and degree of repetition of the words and phrases for each age group have been based on rather careful studies and tests of children's learning processes and the speed with which youngsters of different ages can be expected to learn new words.

Extremely little of this type of work has been done in Latin America. A few countries, particularly Mexico and Puerto Rico, have translated and adapted some North American materials and have done some original work in improving teaching materials for primary schools. Several of the Latin-American countries, however, are still teaching students to read with books similar to those in common use fifty years ago in the United States.

The religious agencies could make a great contribution to elementary education in many of the Latin-American countries through the preparation and introduction of improved teaching materials. The task involved is considerably more than that of translating the books that are used in this country into Spanish or Portuguese. Good translations might, in some instances, be an improvement over existing materials, but there is also the important necessity of adapting the content, as well as the vocabulary, of the books to the cultural setting in which the children live. This, like the problem of improving teaching methods, is a task for an expert, but the task is one which might well be undertaken through a co-operative effort of the United States religious agencies. As a minimum, they should give attention to this problem in the schools which they sponsor.

3. Closely related to the need for improved teaching materials is the

whole problem of testing intelligence and aptitudes and measuring the progress of pupils in their studies. Final examinations are "terribly" important in the Latin-American school system. There is virtually a ritual, carefully prescribed by government regulations in most of the countries, of bringing each student, even those in the kindergarten and first grade, before a board of three examiners at the end of each year to determine whether he should be passed or failed. On the other hand, there is very limited use of tests to guide the teacher in his work with the students.

There are at least three basic functions of a system of tests, only one of which is commonly recognized in most Latin-American schools. First, the results of a well-designed system of intelligence and aptitude tests, when combined with measurements of student progress, provide an important basis for designing a sound curriculum and determining the content of the various courses for different age groups. Second, if the proper tests are given several times during the course of each school year, the results help the teacher to see how effective his methods are and suggest to him changes which he might wisely make in the material which he is presenting, as well as in the methods which he is following. Third, the results of tests are, of course, important in deciding whether individual students should be passed from a lower to a higher—more difficult—level of work. The latter function is exemplified by the "final examination."

The problem of designing, verifying, and standardizing a system of tests that will have meaning in the environment of Latin America requires highly technical skill and ability on the part of experts who are thoroughly acquainted with the culture of the region. Many of the mission schools might well be excellent laboratories in which to do some of the early work that will be necessary. There are many educational psychologists and anthropologists in this country whose talents could be brought to bear on this problem if the religious agencies encouraged their co-operation and used a relatively small amount of funds to cover the expenses of their work.

If a significant number of the religious agencies started creative programs of improving teaching methods, preparing improved textbooks and teaching materials, and developing and standardizing a system of meaningful tests for use with various age groups of school children, they would not only improve their own schools but also make a new contribution to the Latin-American system of education. Efforts in these fields probably require specialists of a type not now found among United States missionaries. The religious agencies, however, could avail themselves of the necessary services if they desired to use funds for these purposes. It is probable that the combined effect of these improvements would be of less immediate importance than a redirection of some of the educational efforts of the religious agencies into technical and vocational areas. Nevertheless, they would make significant and worthwhile additions to the programs of many of the old and well-established institutions. Moreover, they would involve the expenditure of relatively little additional money, and over a period of several years they would bring about some very important changes in the programs of the mission-sponsored schools.

In agricultural activities, there are great variations in both the type and the quality of projects sponsored by the religious agencies. The most common project is a farm which serves as a base for a school, a health service, and an educational program among surrounding farmers. As farms, most of these units are poorly located and poorly managed. A few are profitable, but these are exceptions. Most of them lose money and do little toward introducing improved practices and methods. The schools vary in quality, but most of those which focus attention on practical agricultural subjects, as distinguished from the regular primary and secondary curriculums, appear to be making the greatest contributions. The extension programs with farmers are rarely great successes, but a few make very creditable showings.

The farming operations commonly take an inordinate amount of the agricultural missionary's time. He is too often manager, field foreman, and laborer concurrently. Where the land is poor, which is often the case, the equipment meager, and the labor supply mainly juvenile, the agricultural missionary is so completely enmeshed in running the farm that he has little time for other activities. Many of the religious agencies would greatly improve their agricultural work if they reduced the scale of their farming operations to a 5- to 10-acre truck garden with a very modest amount of good pasture for a few milk cows, hogs, and chickens. This is a type of change which would not only reduce the amount of capital invested and diminish farm operating losses but also allow the agricultural missionary time to develop a community-improvement program in areas near the mission post. It is not, of course, a move that would ordinarily be wise in those rare cases where the present farm is an important source of income for financing non-farming activities.

At those rural mission posts where there is some kind of adult educational work among neighboring farm families—such activities are variously called "agricultural extension," "community development," or "rural leadership" programs—one lesson that has been learned from experience stands out as being universally important: *Little progress was made in these activities as long as they were carried on exclusively by North Americans. National workers, trained and guided by the missionaries, can accomplish much more in getting rural families to improve their farm and home practices than can North Americans.* This principle of employing nationals for extension or community-development work can rather easily be followed in nearly all the Latin-American countries for the simple reason that there are significant numbers of well-trained *agrónomos* or *técnicos* in most of the countries, who can be hired at a modest salary.

In carrying forward the community-improvement programs, it is important that the early emphasis be on promoting a few simple practices that will show fairly immediate results in increased farm income or better family living conditions. In some areas the key practice around which the program can be started is, for example, the construction of trench silos to assure a feed supply for the dry season; the use of new chemicals to kill leaf-cutting ants or other harmful insects; the making and use of compost; the teaching of farm women how to sew and how to make and use a washboard instead of doing the family laundry on rocks along a stream. The particular group of practices around which the community-development program should start will depend on the needs and opportunities within each area. To focus attention on simple practices, however—as contrasted with the organization of co-operatives, herd-improvement associations, organizations to provide irrigation water, or similar community institutions—will ordinarily be an easier starting point and will provide opportunities for the farm families to gain confidence and experience before they tackle more complicated undertakings.

In summary, it can be safely predicted that the religious organizations would greatly improve the quality of their agricultural work in Latin America if they would (1) reduce the scale of their money-losing farming operations; (2) center the attention of their agricultural missionaries on community-improvement programs; (3) employ national technicians to work directly with farm families; and (4) emphasize the adoption of a few simple farm and home practices that will show immediate results in the early stages of each community-development program.

Organization and Administration

In any attempt to evaluate the technical activities of the religious agencies in Latin America, attention must be given to the way in which the missionary enterprise is organized and the prospects which it has of being a continuing and vital source of technical knowledge. In this connection it is well to recognize that each of the sixty-five to seventy religious agencies sponsoring these technical activities in Latin America is an independent and autonomous organization in so far as its technical projects are concerned. Some of the Protestant agencies do not even have the status of an organized church or denomination, and most of the technical work of the various Catholic societies is not subject to any over-all governing body.[5]

In the case of large, well-established denominations, there are three links in the administrative chain of command, of which two are always quite important to technical work. The three are (1) the national church of the denomination in each country to which it sends missionaries; (2) a foreign missions board or council with headquarters and an executive officer in the United States; and (3) the individual missionaries at work in the field. Several Protestant denominations do not have a national church of their own in most Latin-American countries. In these cases the foreign mission board

5. There is a significant degree of co-operation among several of the major Protestant organizations through their affiliation with the Division of Foreign Missions of the National Council of the Churches of Christ in the United States; however, some important Protestant denominations are quite independent of it. Moreover, there is nothing in an agency's affiliation with this division or with analogous organizations, such as the Evangelical Foreign Missions Association or the Interdenominational Foreign Missions Association, which impinges on the responsibility of each of the agencies for its missionaries and the work which they do abroad.

or council in this country and the missionaries abroad are the two important focal points for decision-making. Among Catholic organizations, there is a variation from the Protestant pattern in that there is rarely, if ever, a board or council specializing in foreign mission activities. The "home-office" function is usually performed among the Catholic agencies by a designated officer of each of the missionary organizations.[6]

Where there is a fairly strong national church of a particular denomination in a Latin-American country, its wishes in regard to the number and type of United States missionaries in the country are important. In these cases missionaries are usually assigned to the governing body of the denomination's church in the receiving country. Such assignments, however, are not ordinarily made until there is agreement between the sending and receiving agencies over the number of missionaries and the type of work which each of them is to perform. Among Protestant organizations the sending agency is usually the most important partner to these agreements, because only a few Protestant denominations with strong national churches in Latin America exist, and these affect only a limited number of countries. Moreover, the agencies, among both Catholic and Protestant organizations, appear to determine with a fairly free hand the particular types of projects on which their missionaries will work.

Although the receiving church can never be ignored (and there is considerable variation from country to country and denomination to denomination with respect to its influence), the sending agencies, which are also, of course, the financing agencies, make the important policy decisions about the technical work. It is usually, however, the missionaries in the field who make the management decisions that determine the real nature of particular projects.

The sending agency performs the important functions of helping to raise money, allocating funds among its different activities, selecting personnel for foreign assignments, and giving general adminis-

6. Still another minor variation is found in the case of those Protestant organizations which are not of denominational status. Their foreign posts are usually called "faith missions." Most of them have a "home office" in the United States, which performs some of the same functions as do the foreign mission boards of the established Protestant denominations. Such organizations are rarely of importance in technical service work.

trative guidance to its work abroad. In most cases, however, the missionary, once he is at his foreign post, is left free to develop and carry out a program within the general area of his competence. Quite often, of course, a missionary is hired to direct a particular school, to work at a given hospital, or to operate the farm of a specific rural post, but unless he is assigned as an assistant to the person in charge of a project or particular activity, he develops his own program and goes about his day-to-day work with an absolute minimum of direction and supervision from the headquarters of the sending agency. He commonly corresponds with the "home office" fairly regularly, but he goes for months and in some cases for several years without seeing a responsible officer or staff member of the agency that employs him. Usually, he returns to the United States for one year at the end of each five to seven years of foreign duty. During this one year of home leave he may get a scholarship for study at some college or university, but he commonly spends a good part of the time in fund-raising activities.

As far as the technical work of the religious agencies is concerned, it is roughly accurate to say that the boards and executive officers of the sending agencies generally determine the types and locations of projects, and the missionaries themselves primarily determine the quality of work done at each mission station. The type of project and its location may be important influences on the quality of the work, and the latter in turn may be quite significant in determining the size of a given project. Nevertheless, it is clear that the "home offices" exercise few management functions and the missionaries in the field have relatively little to do with the decisions concerning general policies.

The people who serve on the foreign mission boards and in the executive offices of the sending agencies are rarely trained in a technical subject-matter field. They often have a predisposition to start numerous projects, thereby reaching a large number of people but not the most needy within a given country. The missionaries sent abroad rarely have experienced intensive specialized training pertinent to their activities. A doctor, for instance, is likely to be a general practitioner with ability to do several types of surgery and to administer a hospital. A successful agricultural missionary may have to be a veritable "jack-of-all-trades"; the administrative abili-

ties of a director of a mission-sponsored school may be more important than specialized training in, say, teaching methods. It is, no
doubt, sound personnel policy for the religious agencies to send "the
generalist" instead of the narrowly skilled specialist to the field.

The non-technical interests of the people who determine general
policies, as well as the non-specialized training of many of the missionaries, points up the absence of skilled staff specialists and suggests the need for greater use of technicians to advise the sending
agencies and to assist the field missionaries with their programs of
work. It is doubtful whether either the missionaries or the sending
agencies are commonly kept well informed of changing needs and
new technologies.

Among those Protestant agencies affiliated with the Division of
Foreign Missions of the National Council of the Churches of Christ
in the United States, the deficiency of technical specialists is somewhat offset by the advisory assistance rendered by Agricultural Missions, Inc., World Literacy, Inc., and the Christian Medical Council
for Overseas Work. These assist the committees of the Division of
Foreign Missions in selecting personnel and in counseling individual
missionaries. They act as liaison agents between the missionary
enterprise and the great corps of technicians employed by universities and governments. They promote special training courses in
colleges and universities for missionaries preparing to go abroad or
spending a furlough in the United States. They guide missionaries
in obtaining the technical supplies, equipment, and literature to be
used in Latin America.

The technical services of these three agencies are important, but
they are scanty in proportion to the needs of the religious groups at
work overseas. They reach only part of the Protestant bodies and
almost none of the Catholic agencies. Their staffs are too small to
spend more than a fraction of their time in foreign field work. Their
influence has not been decisive in shaping the type or quality of
the technical assistance work of religious agencies in Latin America.
As pointed out in preceding chapters, the accomplishments of many
missionaries in Latin America might have been multiplied if technical specialists like those employed by these agencies had been "on
the ground" long enough to analyze specific problems.

The technological advances being made in many Latin-American countries, the increasing efforts of governments in education, health, and agriculture, and the large programs of technical assistance sponsored by the United States and the United Nations are important developments which challenge the future significance of the technical work of religious agencies. The day is largely past when a good practical farmer or an ordinary country schoolteacher can go to a mission post in Latin America and make a *national* contribution. There are still thousands of more or less isolated areas in which people of this type can perform very worthy services, and there are scores of submerged groups who are in urgent need of the kinds of assistance that the religious agencies are giving. Nevertheless, if these agencies are to stay in the forefront and are to lead progress, they will almost assuredly have to make much greater use of specialists trained especially in both the social and the natural sciences.

Approaching the problem initially, some of the large denominations might employ two or three specialists, particularly in certain phases of educational and agricultural work where the need is greatest, to work primarily with the missionaries and their superiors. This approach might appeal to the Catholic agencies. Many of them have difficulty in recruiting substantial numbers of good agriculturists because a large proportion of United States Catholics live in urban areas, and relatively few Catholic boys study at agricultural colleges. Another approach might be for a group of agencies to join together in co-operative arrangements for employing highly trained specialists to assist all members of the group. This is essentially the pattern now found among those Protestant agencies that are affiliated with the Division of Foreign Missions and the three technical service agencies previously mentioned—Agricultural Missions, Inc., World Literacy, Inc., and the Christian Medical Council for Overseas Work. Significant expansion and improvement in the quality of the work of these agencies would be a step in the right direction.

Because of denominational differences, both of a doctrinal character and in the scope of foreign technical assistance work, the best approach may well be the establishment of an organization completely outside the ranks of the religious agencies. The presumably excellent technicians of such an organization would serve in a continuing analytical and advisory capacity to all agencies with technical programs abroad. Such a staff would need to have specialists in specific areas of the general fields of education, medicine, and agriculture who could spend a large part of their time in foreign countries working with the missionaries who are faced with the day-to-day problems of project management. Moreover, the individual members of such a staff could hardly be expected to serve on a world-wide basis. Each would need to be a regional, or area, specialist, as well as a subject-matter expert. The establishment and financing of such an organization might well be a significant project for one or more of the large private foundations to undertake.

Finally, worthwhile progress in the continuing task of improving the scientific and technological aspects of the effort can be made by missionaries who develop closer working relationships with the specialists of the United States and the United Nations. This would not be a one-way street, with all the benefit accruing to the religious agencies. Many of the things learned by missionaries can be of real value to the technicians sent to Latin America by the publicly supported agencies.

For instance, several misionaries have learned a great deal about how to work with Indians in Latin America and how to construct hospitals and clinics that best serve the needs of the Indian population. This is a type of information which can be transferred to other technicians. Similarly, there have been new crops and new farming practices tried out by missionaries, some of which have failed and some of which have been successful, but all of which represent a body of experience that can be useful to agriculturists who are now working in the publicly supported programs. There are many illustrations of this kind in which the missionary, on the basis of his experience, has accumulated knowledge which would be valuable to many technicians. There are limits, of course, to the extent to which tax-supported agencies can align themselves with the work of religious agencies, but the limits do not extend to the exchange of scientific information. The representatives of the religious agencies can go much further in most Latin-American countries than they have done in keeping abreast of new ideas and technological developments by keeping in close touch with the subject-matter specialists assigned to secular technical assistance programs. The latter, in turn, have, in those missionaries employed on technical projects, excellent connecting links with the people of the countries in which they are working.

Only by work on many fronts and at all organizational levels can the United States religious agencies in technical work assure themselves of a continuing position abreast of the great social and technological changes that are taking place in Latin America. With their strength partitioned among many independent denominations and organizations, the religious agencies are not in a position to be the pioneers that they have been in the past. Yet it is certainly not beyond their power to make great improvements in their programs. The solid core of past achievements provides a splendid foundation upon which to build.

The spirit of dedicated service to their fellow-man—the greatest asset that any technical program can have—flows strongly in the veins of the missionaries. They are challenged to harness this spirit to sound, up-to-date technical knowledge and to school themselves in the skilled dissemination of this knowledge to the underprivileged millions of common people.

A STATEMENT BY THE NATIONAL PLANNING ASSOCIATION SPECIAL POLICY COMMITTEE ON TECHNICAL CO-OPERATION

For more than half a century churches and religious groups in the United States have been sending missionaries to Latin America. They have been devoting much of their effort to organizing and operating schools and hospitals and other activities which are in many ways similar to those now being undertaken by public agencies in technical co-operation programs. The transfer of technical knowledge and skills was inaugurated by the religious groups long before the United States government or the United Nations and its specialized agencies began their programs.

We believe the study and evaluation prepared by Dr. James G. Maddox is worthy of consideration not only by those who are supporting, administering, and conducting those programs but also by those interested in other programs of technical assistance and co-operation, whether public or private.

Religious groups—Protestant, Catholic, Jewish, interdenominational—have technical assistance programs in every country of Latin America, Dr. Maddox found. These programs are being carried on by 66 different groups; approximately 2,000 missionaries from the United States devote full time to them; and more than $8,000,000 annually are contributed for their support from United States sources alone. Technical assistance work accounts for something like 40 per cent of the total activities of the United States religious groups in Latin America.[1] Education, most of it in primary and secondary schools, receives chief emphasis. Health work, most of it in hospitals and clinics, ranks second, with agriculture third.

The technical assistance work which these missionaries do is different in many respects from that of the technical co-operation

1. Comment by the Rt. Rev. Msgr. L. G. Ligutti: "Dr. Maddox' study covered only the activities of U.S. religious agencies, but it should be remembered that many religious groups and missionaries from countries other than the United States are carrying on similar activities in Latin America."

agencies of the United States government. Nevertheless, for the sake of comparison, it should be pointed out that less than 700 United States nationals were employed in the bilateral programs in Latin America in 1954–55 and that the federal contributions for these totaled over $20,000,000. Thus, in terms of manpower, the activities of the religious groups are nearly three times as great as those of the government, but the dollars available to them are less than half the sums which the government contributes to its own technical co-operation programs in Latin America.

Religious groups now are sponsoring more than 1,000 primary schools in Latin America and about 150 secondary schools. Many of the schools teach only the first three or four grades, but a small number, which started as first-grade schools, have grown until they now offer courses from kindergarten through high school. There is also a considerable number, probably 60, of technical and vocational schools.

In most of the primary and secondary schools the curriculums are those prescribed by the ministries of education in the various countries, and promotion from one grade to another is based on examinations given by representatives of the ministries rather than by the teachers. Almost all the governmentally prescribed curriculums concentrate on the classical subjects—language, mathematics, history, geography, etc.—inherited from Europe a century or more ago. The teaching proceeds by rote, that is, dictation by the teacher, copying and memorizing by the pupil, and regurgitation at examination time. The method of teaching as well as the prescribed curriculums must be followed closely if the pupils in the schools of the religious groups are to pass the examinations required for transfer to other schools or entrance into the colleges or universities. Even so, not all the schools sponsored by the religious groups have adopted this set pattern. Some, without unduly subordinating the established subjects, give the pupil more knowledge of the modern world in which he lives and the problems he will face as a citizen. Some also are introducing improved teaching methods now used in the United States and elsewhere. The technical schools, most of them commercial and vocational, are turning out students with skills and knowledge which are needed, but still scarce, in Latin America.

The missionary medical institutions range from well-equipped and well-staffed modern hospitals to small treatment-rooms in work-ingmen's areas of the cities or at rural mission posts. The latter are sometimes staffed only by a missionary without medical training who gives inoculations and dispenses simple medicines. Some of the hospitals have established schools for nurses' training. The religious groups are bringing medical care to relatively large numbers of people who would not receive it otherwise, but apparently they are introducing few techniques and methods not already known by local doctors. There is great need in Latin America for programs of environmental sanitation, personal hygiene, and preventive medi-cine in general, but only a very small amount of this work is being done by the religious groups.

The churches and religious groups, in addition to teaching voca-tional agriculture in the schools, operate farms and carry on pro-grams of extension education. Most of the farms and extension pro-grams are at the mission centers where schools are located. The farms are used primarily to produce food for the missionaries and students. Some of them have introduced improved strains of live-stock, followed new farming practices, and undertaken experi-mental work, the results of which could be adopted with profit by surrounding farmers. But few of the farms have made significant contributions in these respects, and most are operated at a loss.

Almost all the extension education projects are carried on with the lower-income farmers and consist of donations of small quanti-ties of seeds, assistance in vaccinating livestock, selling insecticides at cost, and explaining their use to individual cultivators. In only rare cases do the programs assist farmers in organizing study groups, encourage the organization of co-operatives, and help farmers tackle their problems through their own collective efforts.

We hope that all representatives of religious groups engaged in planning or conducting technical assistance programs in Latin America will give careful consideration to Dr. Maddox's conclusions and recommendations. The committee has the following conclusions which we believe will make technical assistance efforts more helpful to the people of Latin America and at the same time contribute to the attainment of the ultimate goals of religious groups.

1. We believe that the religious groups have been wise in center-ing their activities in education, health, and agriculture. These are

important fields in which the governments and the people of Latin America still need the assistance of outside agencies. Most of the technical co-operation programs of the United States government in Latin America have been in these same fields, which are also included in the expanded technical assistance programs of the United Nations and the Organization of American States. Thus, historically, the religious groups led the way, and we hope that their technical assistance activities can be increased.[2]

2. It appears to us that the great challenge to the religious groups is to keep their technical assistance programs abreast of the social and technological changes occurring in Latin America. Conditions have changed significantly since religious groups embarked on their technical assistance activities; in many instances fresh approaches are needed. Redirection and reorientation would enhance the effectiveness of programs. The increased emphasis which the Latin-American governments are giving these subjects and the widespread assistance now being rendered by other outside agencies (governmental, intergovernmental, and private) point up the necessity for religious groups to continue their pace-setting and pioneering activities. Religious groups may be in a better position than governmental or intergovernmental agencies to sponsor programs and projects in new fields. Examples are the provision of roads to isolated villages, village schoolhouses or community centers, playing fields and other recreational facilities, cottage industries, and small factories.

3. The effectiveness of many of the programs would be increased if the workers who sponsor and conduct local programs and projects could avail themselves of the services of well-trained specialists in education, health and medical care, agriculture, community organization, and possibly other subjects. These specialists could aid in planning, conducting, and appraising activities. The employees of these religious groups are imbued with a spirit of dedicated service to their fellow-men, the greatest asset for any technical co-operation

2. *Comment by Eric Johnston:* "The needs in elementary and vocational education, and in health and sanitation, are so great in Latin America that every facility should be used for improving them. The religious agencies might well encourage local churches in Latin America, as well as missionaries, to expand their educational and health activities. Religious groups in the United States might offer their services to train Latin-American priests and clergymen in these fields."

or technical assistance effort. Yet all the men and women selected for assignments in Latin America cannot be highly trained in all the phases of their respective fields. Long tours of duty—often in isolated localities—make it difficult for them either to keep abreast of new developments or to appraise objectively the effectiveness of their own efforts. Possibly the religious groups could jointly sponsor a non-denominational and non-sectarian organization which would maintain a staff of highly qualified technicians who would serve in a continuing analytical and advisory capacity for all missionary programs in Latin America.

4. Progress in improving the scientific and technological aspects of the religious groups' programs might be accelerated if closer relationships were established with the workers in the technical cooperation programs of United States and United Nations agencies. Then, too, many things which have been learned by religious groups through their long and varied experience could be of value to the technicians employed by the publicly supported agencies.

5. Educational efforts might be directed toward more children from low-income families. Additional courses in technical and vocational fields might be introduced into the established schools, and new technical and vocational schools might be established, with specialized studies for students who will not or cannot enter the colleges and universities. More and better training might be provided for the teachers, both those from the United States and the nationals of the countries in which the schools are located. This training would include improved teaching methods, the development and use of intelligence and aptitude tests, and the preparation and use of better textbooks and teaching materials. We feel that creative programs in these fields would not only make schools sponsored by religious groups more useful and helpful but also contribute significantly to the Latin-American system of education.

6. In the medical field, more people might be taught simple practices of personal hygiene, good nutrition, home sanitation, and preventive medicine in general. The techniques and methods of preventive medicine are less developed in Latin America than are those of curative medicine. Creative programs in selected areas could lead the way toward widespread improvement.

7. The unprofitable farming operations designed to produce food for the mission stations, schools, and hospitals might be curtailed or even abandoned, and activities redirected toward community improvement programs. In such programs nationals of the host country rather than United States technicians might well be employed to work directly with the rural people; in the beginning of a community program, emphasis might well be placed on simple farm and home practices giving immediate results.

8. The committee believes that it is especially important for the Latin American governments and peoples to recognize the notable contributions which these technical assistance activities of the religious groups have made to economic development.

9. Finally, it is our hope that Dr. Maddox's report will add knowledge to the substantial role which religious groups have played in the development of the concept of technical co-operation and that it will contribute generally to public understanding of the gains that can be made through a sharing of knowledge and skills.

131

DAVID J. WINTON, Chairman of the Board, Winton Lumber Company

MRS. LOUISE LEONARD WRIGHT, Midwest Director, Institute of International Education

OBED A. WYUM, Farm Program Consultant, Farmers Union

ARNOLD S. ZANDER, International President, American Federation of State, County and Municipal Employees

★   ★   ★

JOHN MILLER, *Assistant Chairman and Executive Secretary of the National Planning Association and of the Policy Committee*

APPENDIX A

NPA PUBLICATIONS POLICY

The National Planning Association is an independent, non-political, non-profit organization established in 1934. It is an organization where leaders of agriculture, business, labor, and the professions join in programs to maintain and strengthen private initiative and enterprise.

Those who participate in the activities of NPA believe that the tendency to break up into pressure groups is one of the gravest disintegrating forces in our national life. America's number-one problem is that of getting diverse groups to work together for this objective: To combine our efforts to the end that the American people may always have the highest possible cultural and material standard of living without sacrificing their freedom. Only through joint democratic efforts can programs be devised which support and sustain each other in the national interest.

NPA's Standing Committees—the Agriculture, Business, and Labor Committees on National Policy and the Committee on International Policy—and its Special Committees are assisted by a permanent research staff. Whatever their particular interests, members have in common a fact-finding and socially responsible attitude.

NPA believes that through effective private planning we can avoid a "planned economy." The results of NPA's work will not be a grand solution to all our ills. But the findings, and the process of work itself, will provide concrete programs for action on specific problems, planned in the best traditions of a functioning democracy.

NPA's publications—whether signed by its Board, its Committees, its staff, or by individuals—are issued in an effort to pool different knowledges and skills, to narrow areas of controversy, and to broaden areas of agreement.

All reports published by NPA have been examined and authorized for publication under policies laid down by the Board of Trustees. Such action does not imply agreement by NPA Board or Committee members with all that is contained therein, unless such endorsement is specifically stated.

133

APPENDIX B

LEON HENDERSON, Chief Economist, Research Institute of America, Inc.

ERIC JOHNSTON, President, Motion Picture Association of America, Inc.

FRED LAZARUS, JR., President, Federated Department Stores, Inc.

MURRAY D. LINCOLN, President, Farm Bureau Mutual Insurance Companies

DAVID L. LUKE, JR., President, West Virginia Pulp and Paper Company

JAMES G. PATTON, President, National Farmers Union

CLARENCE E. PICKETT, Honorary Secretary, American Friends Service Committee

WALTHER P. REUTHER, President, Congress of Industrial Organizations

JOHN V. RIFFE, Executive Vice-President, Congress of Industrial Organizations

*ELMO ROPER, Elmo Roper, Marketing

*THEODORE W. SCHULTZ, Chairman, Department of Economics, University of Chicago

HERMAN W. STEINKRAUS, President, Bridgeport Brass Company

CHARLES J. SYMINGTON, Chairman of the board, The Symington-Gould Corporation

ROBERT C. TAIT, President, Stromberg-Carlson Company

JOHN HAY WHITNEY, J. H. Whitney & Company

DAVID J. WINTON, Chairman of the board, Winton Lumber Company

J. D. ZELLERBACH, President, Crown Zellerbach Corporation

INDEX

Administration and organization of technical assistance programs, recommendations on, 118–24

Agricultural Missions, Inc., 121, 122

Agricultural programs of religious organizations: Andean Indians, 75–85; farms, 38–39; general description of, 38–40, 73–74; number of projects by country, 38; recommendations, 116–18; schools and colleges, 35–36, 96–99

American ORT Federation, schools, 62–63

Andean Indians: account of, 74–85; agricultural programs with, 75–85; educational programs with, 76, 78; land distribution for, 81–82; medical programs with, 76, 79; problem of, 83–85

Baptist church, health programs, 64–67

Baptist Hospital; *see* Hospital Bautista

Benedictine priests, schools of, 44–47

Bolivia: agricultural programs, 74, 80–82; educational programs, 42–44, 49–50; programs visited, 2

Brazil: agricultural colleges, 96–99; educational programs, 52–55, 59–61; programs visited, 2

Buitrón, Anibal, 8 ff.

Calderón Indians, agricultural programs with, 77–80

Camohmila Rural Center; *see* Centro Rural de Camohmila

Canadian Baptists, 81

Capuchin priests, 55–56

Centro Rural de Camohmila, Mexico, 90–96, 103

Chile: agricultural programs, 86–89; health programs, 68–70; programs visited, 3

Christian Brothers, educational programs, 55–69

Christian Medical Council for Overseas Work, 121, 122

Church of the Brethren, Foreign Mission Commission of, agricultural programs, 77–80

Church of England, 56

Clínica Adventista, Paraguay, 68

Colegio Internacional, Paraguay, 47–49

Colegio San José, Nicaragua, 55–59, 63, 64, 105

Colegio del Tepeyac, Mexico, 44–47, 49

Committee on Co-operation in Latin America, 75 ff.

Conclusions and recommendations: efficiency, 102–9; general, 100–124; need for specialists, 121–23; organizational, 118–24; quality of performance, 109–18

Co-operation with governmental and international organizations, 123

Co-operation among religious agencies, 75–77, 118 ff., 121

Disciples of Christ, educational programs, 47–49

Economy and levels of living in Latin America, 14–18

Ecuador, agricultural programs, 74–80

Educational activities of religious organizations: commercial schools, 52; cultural forces influencing, 10, 30, 31, 41, 43, 45–46, 48–49, 102; general description of, 29–36; high schools, 52; Latin-American governments and, 32–33, 104; methods of instruction, 32; number and type of schools sponsored by religious agencies, 29; preparatory schools, 45–47;